100 Hikes in™
WASHINGTON'S
ALPINE LAKES

SECOND EDITION

100 Hikes in™
WASHINGTON'S ALPINE LAKES

SECOND EDITION

Vicky Spring, Ira Spring
& Harvey Manning

The Mountaineers • Seattle

5 4 3 2
5 4 3 2 1

Published by The Mountaineers
1011 SW Klickitat Way, Seattle, Washington 98134

Published simultaneously in Canada by Douglas & McIntyre, Ltd., 1615 Venables Street, Vancouver, B.C. V5L 2H1

Published simultaneously in Great Britain by Cordee, 3a DeMontfort Street, Leicester, England, LE1 7HD

Manufactured in the United States of America

Edited by Dana Fos
Maps by Helen Sherman
Photographs by Bob and Ira Spring and Kirkendall/Spring
Book design by Marge Mueller
Typesetting by The Mountaineers Books

Cover photograph: Sprite Lakelet and Prusik Peak, Enchantment Lakes region
Frontispiece: Gnome Tarn and Prusik Peak (Hike 20)
Page 6: Lila Lake and Hibox Mountain (Hike 79)

Library of Congress Cataloging in Publication Data
Spring, Vicky. 1953–
        100 Hikes in Washington's Alpine Lakes / Vicky Spring, Ira Spring & Harvey Manning. -- 2nd ed.
            p.   cm.
        Rev. ed. of: 100 hikes in the Alpine Lakes. c1985
        Includes index.
        ISBN 0-89886-306-6
        1. Hiking--Washington (State)--Alpine Lakes Wilderness--Guidebooks.
2. Alpine Lakes Wilderness (Wash.)--Guidebooks. I. Spring, Ira. II. Manning, Harvey. III. Spring, Vicky, 1953–
100 hikes in the Alpine Lakes. IV. Title. V. Title: One hundred hikes in Washington's Alpine Lakes.
GV199.42.W22A477 1993
917.97--dc20   92-41915
                                         CIP

CONTENTS

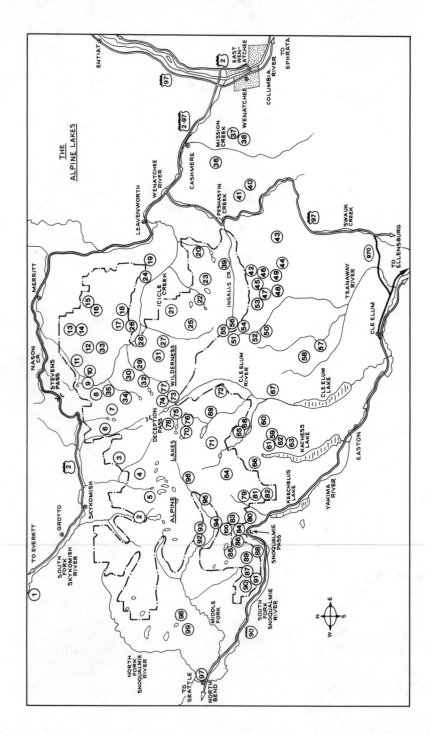

6

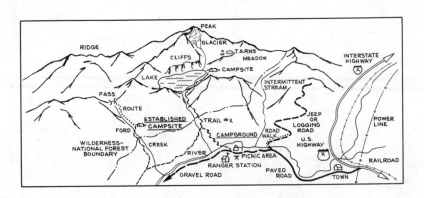

Yellow bells bloom at the edge of receding east-Cascades snowbanks

IS THERE ROOM IN THE WORLD FOR BOOTS?

A Nostalgic Look Back and a Quizzical Look Ahead

A half-century ago, when we, the authors of this book, already had outgrown and worn out many pairs of hiking boots, the mountain wilderness of Washington was traversed and crisscrossed and circled and looped by thousands of miles of trails. However, even as we grew from rambling Boy Scouts to peakbagging Mountaineers, roads were thrusting up pristine valleys, climbing over forest ridges, chewing up and spitting out the bootways that had existed long before we came to them. Then, as we were maturing into less kinetic and more reflective birdwatchers and flowersniffers, our backcountry meditations were disrupted by the "off-road vehicle," or ORV, a Yankee-Japanese ingenuity designed to exploit the remaining legacy of foot/horse trails as runways for motor-driven wheels. The term off-road vehicle is an oxymoron, and so, too, is "motorcycle trail." A route traveled by machines is not a *trail,* it is a *road.* The Forest Service was slow to learn that the vast majority of hikers will not walk on a road, whether traveled by four wheels or merely two. To put wheels on a trail (and this applies to bicycles as well as motorcycles) is to take it away from pedestrians.

By the 1960s we had lost a third of our inherited trail miles to logging roads and ORVs. To avoid losing everything, hikers sought the designation of much of our best trail country as national wilderness, areas from which roads and machines are excluded. The wilderness concept embodies our highest aspirations to be worthy stewards of Mother Earth. The heart of the concept—the *soul*—is self-denial of selfish self-gratification, whether for economic gain—or for *recreational pleasure.* In an area dedicated to wilderness preservation, recreation must take second place to preservation of the natural systems in order to keep intact not only the ecological integrity but the recreational quality. Because too much of modern civilization follows no higher moral principle than "if it feels good, do it," wilderness regulations are necessary to teach the newcomer the natural law that it is his duty to self-enforce. Only thus can the wilderness be kept *wild.*

Now comes the crunch.

The state's population has approximately doubled since the 1960s; just as we then prophesied, hikers here overwhelmed the dedicated wilderness areas. Many sites are being overpopulated to the point of destruction. This cannot be allowed to continue. But what of the "surplus" hikers? Belatedly, the Forest Service is trying to find alternative trails to which it can steer the trammeling throngs, without much luck. Action should have been taken when the problem first became visible on the far (then) horizon. It was not. And so the crunch.

Through the 1960s, 1970s, and 1980s, the Forest Service bitterly resisted wilderness designation, arguing that it should be left to manage crowds free from wilderness restrictions, such as those banning power tools and discouraging "hardened" campsites and large-capacity sanitary facilities. But when it succeeded in excluding lands from wilderness, how did it exercise administrative freedom? By converting trails to roads, if not for logging then for ORVs and—now—for bicycles.

Most egregiously, in the 1960s when hikers were few and trails plentiful, Wenatchee National Forest allocated 900 miles of trails east of the Alpine Lakes Wilderness to motorized use. Most nonwilderness trails in that area became motorized, no consideration given to what their best use might be. Many have magnificent scenery and other appeals, but a motorcycle so shatters the experience sought by hikers that most will not walk where they might encounter the racket and the stench. We do not claim these east-side trails equal the spectacular lake country of the Alpine Lakes Wilderness, but when all the wilderness trails are full they are not bad, not bad at all. Many ought to be returned to hikers, the ORVers then provided new trails better suited to their high-speed travel. Let Wenatchee National Forest rangers know what you think.

The western side of the Alpine Lakes Wilderness, a hop and a skip from downtown Seattle, presents a different challenge. The most severe overuse of the wilderness occurs there, some 35 favorite sites documented at more than 300 percent of endurable impact. In the area adjoining the wilderness, ORVers are relatively few. As are hikers. Because so are trails. Yet the "wildland" of this fringe area offers many of the satisfactions of the "wilderness experience." A new system of trails and campsites is wanted there. A highline from Mt. Si to Mt. Teneriffe to Green Mountain to Bessemer Mountain, and another from Garcia (Mailbox) Peak to Bandera Mountain, and another from Rattlesnake Mountain to Mt. Washington to McClellans Butte to Snoqualmie Pass would add innumerable "classics" (or semi-classics, at least) to the hiker's treasury. The valley trail up the Middle Fork Snoqualmie River discussed later in these pages, and a trail on the opposite side of the valley, following the route of the historic CCC Truck Road, would tie the highlines together and would, in their own right, provide year-round hiking and camping. Such a system could absorb more hikers/campers than the whole of the Alpine Lakes Wilderness in that overused "hour from downtown Seattle" zone.

And that is only the start. Fortunately, within an hour's drive of downtown Seattle are areas in the Mt. Baker–Snoqualmie National Forest that have superb alpine lakes, meadows, and views equal to those in the Alpine Lakes Wilderness—but that, for various reasons (including logging roads), are not on conservationists' list of proposed new wilderness. Pour over the 7.5-minute maps of the Pratt River (USGS Lake Philippa, Bandera), Ragged Ridge (USGS Mt. Stickney, Monte Cristo, Index), Eagle Rock (USGS Baring, Evergreen Mtn.), and Mt. Dickerman (USGS Helena Ridge, Silverton, Bedal). To be sure, portions of all these areas *are* proposed for new wilderness, but others are not. Look at the meadows and lakes shown on these maps and decide where you would put trails to relieve the impact of overuse in the wilderness. Let Mt. Baker–Snoqualmie National Forest rangers know what you decide.

Meanwhile, when you arrive at a trailhead parking lot full to overflow-

Deception Creek (Hike 6)

ing and calculate the number of boots loosed by the mass of cars, you may decide to try elsewhere. At the end of this book is a list of "dispersal trails." They aren't the Enchantments or Robin Lakes but neither are they booby prizes. Try them.

The destruction of trails was a central motivation of the National Wilderness Act of 1964. A partial listing of what the concept has so far given us in Washington: the Glacier Peak Wilderness of 1960 gained statutory guarantees; the North Cascades National Park Act of 1968 set aside, besides the park, the Lake Chelan and Ross Lake National Recreation Areas, Pasayten Wilderness, and additions to the Glacier Peak Wilderness; in 1976 came the Alpine Lakes Wilderness; in 1984 the Washington Wilderness Act, encompassing more than 1,000,000 acres of national forests; and in 1988 the Washington Parks Wilderness Act safeguarding the heartlands of Mt. Rainier, Olympic, and North Cascades National Parks.

For all this, the wilderness system of the state is by no means complete. In 1984 the conservation community submitted a proposal to protect 3,000,000 acres, omitting about that many more deserving acres for the sake of "practicality." The 1,000,000 acres granted protection in 1984 were a joy to behold, yet while filling the glass one-third full, Congress left it two-thirds empty. The citizen efforts that were partial victories in 1960, 1964, 1968, 1976, 1984, and 1988 must look ahead to the next objectives.

The Alpine Lakes Wilderness of 1976 was sabotaged generations before the idea of it was born. The Northern Pacific Land Grant of 1864 gave enormous tracts of wildland to private investors to finance construction of the railroad; the bulk of these privatized lands never were touched by the railroad builders, nor by any exploiter until the recent past, when the logging moved from lowlands to mountains. Around the entire periphery of the Alpine Lakes Wilderness are privately held square-mile blocks of the railroad-grant "checkerboard," in acreage at least equalling that of the dedication, which deserve preservation. Examples are Icicle Ridge, extending from the edge of Leavenworth to highlands of the Mormon Lakes; the approach to McCue Ridge and Chiwaukum Creek; the Pratt River; the Teanaway River; and the ridge from Blewett Pass to Ingalls Peak. Our next objectives . . . .

Something Wicked This Way Comes

The machine. The wheel.

Now, hold on a minute, all ye slickly professional quoters-out-of-context. Back off and listen to the whole story. We wilderness preservers are quite aware that without the can-opener we'd be flinging tin cans off cliffs, in the manner of gulls carrying clams high in the air to crack the shells open by dropping them on beach rocks. We know full well that without the wheel the barrow would have to be a travois or a sled.

The machine and the wheel are indispensable to our civilization. But, except possibly for the Swiss Army knife, machines are out of place in wilderness. (For wheels there is that one exception, the muscle-powered wheelbarrow.)

The U.S. Forest Service has an institutional blind spot. It does not recognize the difference between a trail and a road. —Make that *two* blind spots. It considers all means of travel, by foot or wheel, by musclepower or internal-combustion engine, equal. (Except, as in Orwell's novel *Animal Farm,* "some are more equal than others," the "some" comprising in this case those that are most technologically advanced.)

While conservationists were busy saving Washington trails, creating a new national park and a bouquet of new wildernesses, the Forest Service was assiduously converting *true trails* (that is, paths suitable for speeds of up to 5 or so miles per hour, the pace of a horse) to *motorcycle roads* (that is, motorways designed to let the ORV do 15–30 miles per hour). During a quarter-century in which the concerted efforts of tens of thousands of conservationists protected large expanses of wildland from invasion by machines, a comparative handful of ORVers succeeded in converting more miles of trails to de facto roads than the conservationists saved. Only 45 percent (1985 count) of Washington trails are machine-free by virtue of being in national parks and wildernesses; of the other 55 percent, located in multiple-use areas of national forests, half are open to motorcycles. In other words, 27½ percent of Washington trails have been converted to ORV roads. Do ORVers comprise 27½ percent of backcountry travelers? No, only about 4 percent.

When automobiles arrived in America, the citizenry and government were quick to see they should not be permitted on sidewalks. The Forest Service is slower to recognize that the difference in speed and purpose between motorized wheels and muscle-powered feet are irreconcilable. Thinking to serve the laudable purpose of supplying "a wide spectrum of recreational opportunities," the Forest Service initially tolerated ORVers, then began encouraging them, widening and straightening and smoothing "multiple-use trails" (still another oxymoron) to permit higher speeds, thus increasing the number of motors and discouraging hikers, thus establishing single-purpose *ORV-roads.*

Federal funds were employed for the conversion until that source dried up; since 1979 the Forest Service has relied heavily on money from the State of Washington Interagency for Outdoor Recreation (IAC), an agency that is dominated by "multiple-users" with a strong lean toward wheels.

The resulting and ongoing mass conversion of trails to roads could not happen if hikers were given the respect their numbers—overwhelming compared to the motorcyclists—deserve. Hikers spoke up for the Washington Wilderness Act of 1984. By many thousands they wrote letters to congressmen and senators, submerging the opposition voice of road-builders and ORVers. The pen is mightier than the wheel, and it must be taken up again, by those same tens of thousands, to write letters to congressmen and senators, with copies to the Regional Forester, Region 6, U.S.F.S., 319 S.W. Pine Street, P.O. Box 3623, Portland, Oregon 97208, asking the following:

1. Trails be considered a valuable resource, treated as a separate category in all forest plans.
2. All trail-users should be notified of public meetings concerning any forest plan affecting trails; public meetings should be held in metropolitan areas as well as in small, remote communities near the trails.
3. To help reduce the conflict between hikers and ORVers, hikers on "multiple-use trails" (often with little children and heavy packs) shall have the right-of-way. For the safety of both parties, a speed limit about halfway between those of a swift hiker and a middling-fast horse shall be enforced on all "multiple-use trails." We do not concede that a "multiple-use trail" is a trail at all, but these measures can help reduce the present danger, pending philosophical retraining of land-managers.

And Then the Silent Violence

The National Wilderness Act, wiser than the Forest Service, distinguishes between a footway—a trail—and a wheelway—a road. The act bans from trails not merely the motorized but the *mechanized,* which means wheels. Bicycles—"mountain bikes"—are not permitted for the simple reason that in appropriate terrain they readily can do 5–10 miles per hour, an obscenely excessive speed when mingled with the 1–3 miles per hour of the traveler on foot.

Routes exist outside dedicated wilderness—logging roads, jeep roads, sheep driveways, and the like—that can be amicably shared by bicycles and pedestrians; thousands of miles of these may quite appropriately be considered "multi-use routes" (*not trails*). However, the more kinetic bikers disdain such routes and seek "equal rights" on what they refer to as "single-track" trails (that is, trails built over the decades by and for hikers and horses). Unfortunately, what these bikers consider "equality" is the status enjoyed by the pigs who rule Orwell's *Animal Farm;* when feet and wheels meet on a "single track," the wheels inevitably are "more equal."

The new breed of bicycle is an excellent machine and deserves a spacious place in the spectrum of outdoor recreations. However, it does not belong on each and every trail, and it cannot establish a niche for itself by driving pedestrians from their trails—and make no mistake, there can be no friendly, safe "sharing" of a single-track trail by people walking 1–3 miles per hour and cyclists who on the downhill "bombing runs" that are the quintessence of their sport are discontented by any speed slower than 15–25 miles per hour.

As could have been predicted, the Forest Service welcomed the new use and instantly opened to bicycles hundreds of miles of single-track trails, with never a whisper about public hearings. The agency's multiple-use philosophy is the modern equivalent of the medieval method of settling feline disputes—dumping all the cats in a gunnysack and leaving them alone to fight it out.

There has to be a better way, one that will permit hikers and bikers to coexist—partly on readily shared multi-use routes, but where single-track travel is desired, *on separate routes.* Few single-track bikeways exist; they must be newly built. It must be up to the bikers who invest many hundreds of dollars in their wheels and gear and garb to take the lead in financing this construction, to build bikeways as generations of boots have built trails. The nonbiking public cannot be expected to shoulder this very heavy financial burden.

Must Each Man Kill the Thing He Loves?

In the 1960s The Mountaineers began publishing trail guides as another means of working "to preserve the natural beauty of Northwest America." We suffered no delusion that large numbers of boots improve trails or enhance wildness. However, we had learned to our rue that "you use it or lose it," that threatened areas could only be saved if they were more widely known and treasured.

Our first *100 Hikes* saved a number of trails from census and wheels. So successful were we in peopling threatened trails that those new hikers who had not been (as had we) in the backcountry before the population explosion began (when Johnny came marching home from World War II and married Jenny) accused us of generating the mobs of new boots, ignoring the activities of Johnny and Jenny. Whoever or whatever was the villain in the piece, we all felt a deep concern for the dwindling of solitude and the accompanying increase in land-trashing. To disperse the boots and sleeping bags and thereby relieve the pressure on fragile ecosystems, we expanded *100 Hikes* to five volumes, a series that now describes virtually every major trail in the Cascades and Olympics—and in the Alpine Lakes, a great many lesser trails as well.

Dispersal is effective when there are places to send the surplus boots. However, the Alpine Lakes Wilderness, the "backyard wilderness" of a population that has doubled since publication of our first *100 Hikes,* is running out of spare room. When all its trails and campsites are full up, where will the hikers go?

Obviously the wilderness must be enlarged to the boundaries that should have been established in 1976. However, preservation of wilderness ecosystems from over-use entails regulations to limit the number of boots, such as by requiring a permit, and to reduce the number of sleeping bags, such as by designating certain scenic climaxes "Day Use Only." A larger wilderness is essential but cannot by itself do what is needed.

Surrounding the Alpine Lakes Wilderness (by which we mean the Wilderness-That-Should-Be-and-Will-Become) is a "wilderness-fringe" backcountry whose potential for increased, and enhanced, trail recreation is very great. The richest opportunity is on the east. In the 1960s, hikers few and lonesome trails abundant, Wenatchee National Forest allocated 900 miles of trails to motorcycles. The views and forests and flowers and streams on these routes were (and are) superb, yet hikers quickly abandoned them. Why? Because they found even the briefest confrontation with racketing and reeking and racing motors totally mood-shattering, trip-wrecking. Ironically, many of the routes the Forest Service gave motorcyclists are so unsuited to the recreation sought by these worthies as to hardly ever hear a motor or see a wheel. Some of the lonesomest trails in the Cascades are those signed for motorcycles! The rangers of the 1960s didn't understand hikers; neither did they understand ORVers. To be sure, ORVers are as loud in their lobbying as in their recreation and will howl in rage at any suggestion their share of trails be reduced. But they are a tiny minority compared to the (presently) silent majority of hikers. Wenatchee National Forest is going to have to adjust its hearing aid.

Grindstone Mountain from Upper Florence Lake (Hike 33)

INTRODUCTION

The country sampled by these 100 hikes has many characteristics in common throughout. Most notably, past glaciation has left in all parts a legacy of sharp-sculptured peaks, plus cirque basins and scoured valleys now filled by lakes high and low—some 600 in all. However, the area is divided in two quite radically different sections: west and east. On windward slopes of the Cascades, the maritime side, the precipitation is heavy enough to nourish virtual rain forests. The leeward slopes, in the rainshadow, often are sunny when the crest is lost in mists and drizzles, and the forests generally more open.

The hiking season in low-elevation valleys is almost the whole year; higher, the flowers may not poke through snowbanks until late July, a mere several weeks before their frozen seeds are blanketed by the new winter's white; higher still, there are no flowers ever, and no real hiking season, either, only a climbing season. There are places on the east slopes where on any day of the year a person has an excellent chance of a sunburn, and others, on the west slope, where on any day of the year a person has a good chance of getting soaking wet right through his rainproof parka, and others, on the Cascade Crest, where hikers within a mile of each other are at one and the same time gasping from thirst (east) and sputtering like a whale (west).

Administration

The Alpine Lakes area is administered by the U.S. Forest Service in the Mt. Baker–Snoqualmie and Wenatchee National Forests. A large portion of the region is in the Alpine Lakes Wilderness, where "the earth and its community of life are untrammeled by man, where man himself is a visitor who does not remain." Motorized travel (and mechanized travel, including "mountain bikes") are forbidden absolutely and horse travel is carefully regulated or at some points eliminated; foot travel and camping are receiving increasing regulatory attention to eliminate or minimize human impact.

A study of the administration of the wilderness is expected to be completed by 1993–94, probably resulting in some sort of permit system.

Maps and Current Information

Each hike description in this book lists the most useful topographic maps, which usually is the Green Trails modification of the base map produced by the U.S. Geological Survey (USGS). On these privately published sheets, obsolete information (trails that no longer exist) is edited out and surviving trails delineated by a green-ink overlay. Updated versions are issued every two years. Both the Green Trails and USGS sheets are sold at mountain equipment and map shops.

The national forests publish recreation maps that are quite accurate and up-to-date. These may be obtained for a small fee at ranger stations or by writing the forest supervisors:

Mt. Baker–Snoqualmie National Forest
21905 64th Ave. West
Mountlake Terrace, Washington 98043

Wenatchee National Forest
P.O. Box 811
Wenatchee, Washington 98801

Neither maps nor guidebooks can keep up with changes by nature and man. When current information about a certain trail is sought, the hiker should visit or telephone the Forest Service ranger station listed in the text. Following are addresses and phone numbers:

North Bend Ranger District
North Bend, Washington 98045
(206) 888-1421

Skykomish Ranger District
Skykomish, Washington 98288
(206) 677-2414

Lake Wenatchee Ranger District
Star Route, Box 109; Leavenworth, Washington 98826
(509) 763-3103 or -3211

Leavenworth Ranger District
600 Sherbourne; Leavenworth, Washington 98826
(509) 548-5817 or 782-1413

Cle Elum Ranger District
West 2nd; Cle Elum, Washington 98922
(509) 674-4411

Maps

The sketch maps in this book are intended to give only a general idea of the terrain and trails. Once out of the city and off the highways, the navigation demands precision.

In the 1980s the Forest Service renumbered their roads. A veteran traveler relying on his faithful file of well-worn Forest Service maps had best never leave civilization without a full tank of gas, survival rations, and instructions to family or friends on when to call out the Logging Road Search and Rescue Team. If maps are older than ten years, a party would do better to obtain the current National Forest recreation maps, which are cumbersome for the trail but essential to get about on the renumbered roads.

The new U.S. Forest Service system of road numbers gives main roads two numerals. For example, the Foss River road is No. 68 and is shown on the Forest Service maps as 68 and described in this guidebook as road No. 68. The secondary roads have the first two numbers of the main road plus two additional numbers. For example, from road 68 the secondary road to Tonga Ridge is 6830, and it is shown on Forest Service maps as 6830. Three additional numbers are added for a spur road. The Tonga Ridge trailhead road becomes 6830310, shown as ⟨310 on Forest Service maps, 310 on Forest Service signs, and as road No. (6830)310 in this guidebook.

These maps may be obtained for a fee at ranger stations or by writing Forest Supervisors at:

Mt. Baker–Snoqualmie National Forest
21905 64th Ave. West; Mountlake Terrace, Washington 98043

Wenatchee National Forest
P.O. Box 811; Wenatchee, Washington 98801

Also available from ranger stations, as well as from map shops and sporting goods stores, is the Alpine Lakes Wilderness map.

The best maps in the history of the world are the topographic sheets produced by the U.S. Geological Survey (USGS), and these, too, are sold by map shops and sporting goods stores. However, revision is so occasional that information on roads and trails is always largely obsolete. Essential as they are for off-trail, cross-country explorers, in this book we have recommended them only when there is no alternative.

As it happens, among the merits of the USGS is that it sells the data "separations" (from which its sheets are made) on a nonprofit, cost-only, public-service basis. This has enabled commercial publishers to buy the separations, add and delete information, and issue maps that are designed specifically for hikers and kept up to date. Though the USGS base map is always available, for areas where they exist we recommend the maps in the Green Trails series, which covers virtually all hiking areas in the Cascades and Olympics, and the Custom Correct series for the Olympics.

Clothing and Equipment

Northwest mountain weather, especially on the ocean side of the ranges, is notoriously undependable. Cloudless morning skies can be followed by afternoon deluges of rain or fierce squalls of snow. Even without a storm a person can get mighty chilly on high ridges when—as often happens—a cold wind blows under a bright sun and pure blue sky.

No one should set out on a Cascade trail, unless for a brief stroll, lacking warm long pants, wool (or the equivalent) shirt or sweater, and a windproof and rain-repellent parka, coat, or poncho. (All these in the rucksack, if not on the body during the hot hours.) And on the feet, sturdy shoes or boots plus two pair of wool socks and an extra pair in the pack.

As for that rucksack, it should also contain the Ten Essentials, found to be so by generations of members of The Mountaineers, often from sad experience:

1. Extra clothing—more than needed in good weather.
2. Extra food—enough so something is left over at the end of the trip.
3. Sunglasses—necessary for most alpine travel and indispensable on snow.
4. Knife—for first aid and emergency firebuilding (making kindling).
5. Firestarter—a candle or chemical fuel for starting an emergency fire with wet wood.
6. First-aid kit.
7. Matches—in a waterproof container.
8. Flashlight—with extra bulb and batteries.
9. Map—be sure it's the right one for the trip.
10. Compass—be sure to know the declination, east or west.

Camping and Fires

A single small party may trample subalpine grass, flowers, and heather so badly they don't recover for several years. If the same spot is used several or more times a summer, year after year, the greenery vanishes, replaced by bare dirt. The respectful traveler always aims to camp in the woods or in rocky morainal areas. These alternatives lacking, it is better to use a meadow site already bare and accepted by the land-managers as a "sacrifice area" rather than extend the destruction into virginal places nearby. However, at popular camps the "sacrifice" has obliterated so much meadow the site has lost most of the beauty that made it popular. Meadow rehabilitation projects aim to restore that beauty by revegetation. Lovers of the land will want to cooperate fully and joyfully.

Particularly to be avoided are camps on soft meadows on the banks of streams and lakes. These may endanger the water purity as well as the delicate plants. Moreover, a camp on a waterside viewpoint makes the beauty unavailable to other hikers who simply want to stop for a look, or lunch, and then go camp in the woods. Carry a collapsible water container to minimize the trips to the water supply that beat down a path. (As a bonus, the container lets you camp high on a dry ridge, where the solitude and the views are.) Carry a lightweight pair of camp shoes, less destructive to plants and soils than trail boots.

As laissez-faire camping gives way to thoughtful management, different policies are being adopted in different places. For example, high-use spots may be designated "Day Use Only," forbidding camps. In others there may be a blanket rule against camps within 100 or 200 feet of water. The rule everywhere is always to use officially *designated* sites and, in their absence, to use *established* sites; wilderness rangers on their rounds dis-establish those sites judged unacceptable.

Never ditch tent or tarp unless and until essential to avoid being flooded out—and afterward be sure to fill the ditches, carefully replacing any sod that may have been dug up. Always carry a sleeping pad of some sort to keep your bag dry and your bones comfortable. Do not revert to the ancient bough bed of the frontier past.

The wood fire also is next to obsolete in the high country. At best, dry firewood is hard to find at popular camps. What's left, the picturesque silver snags and logs, is part of the scenery, too valuable to be wasted cooking a pot of soup. Needless to say, green, living wood must never be cut; it doesn't burn anyway.

Both for reasons of convenience and conservation, the highland hiker should carry a lightweight stove for cooking (or else should not cook—though the food is cold, the inner man is hot) and depend on clothing and shelter for warmth. The pleasures of a roaring blaze on a cold mountain night are indisputable, but a single party on a single night may use up ingredients of the scenery that were many human lifetimes in growing, dying, and silvering.

Where campfires are allowed, do not make a new fire ring—use an existing one. In popular areas patrolled by rangers, its existence means this is an approved, "designated," or "established" campsite. Use only dead and down wood. When finished, be certain the fire is absolutely out—drown the coals and stir them with a stick and then drown the ashes until the smoking and steaming have stopped completely and a finger stuck

Turquoise Lake (Hike 30)

in the slurry feels no heat. Embers can smoulder underground in dry duff for days, spreading gradually and burning out a wide pit—or kindling trees and starting a forest fire. If a fire ring has been heaped over with rocks, it means the site has been dis-established.

A final word on camping in the Alpine Lakes Wilderness: maybe you should think it over. A night's stay at a beauty spot, no matter how assiduous the attention to "no trace," has an impact a dozen or more times greater than a day-hike lunch stop. Wilderness nights are too deeply magical to be foregone. However, the nights at certain places may have to be given up in order to preserve the magic of the days. Furthermore, hikers must start thinking in terms of "sharing." Many a long-time backpacker has altogether quit camping in, for example, Mt. Rainier National Park, saying, "Well, I guess I've *had* my share of *that*." In the Alpine Lakes the rule (a moral, not a legal, imperative) should be considered for the Enchantments, Robin Lakes, Mormon Lakes, and for other super-spectaculars, super-populars. A once-in-a-lifetime experience.

Water

No open water ever, nowadays, can be considered certainly safe for human consumption. Any reference in this book to "drinking water" is not a guarantee. It is entirely up to the individual to judge the situation.

In the late 1970s began a great epidemic of giardiasis, caused by a vicious little parasite that spends part of its life cycle swimming free in water and part in the intestinal tract of beavers and other wildlife, dogs, and people. Actually the "epidemic" was solely in the press; *Giardia* were first identified in the eighteenth century and are present in the public water systems of many cities of the world and many towns in America—including some in the foothills of the Cascades. Long before the "outbreak" of "beaver fever," there was the well-known malady, the "Boy Scout trots." This is not to make light of the disease; though most humans feel no ill effects (but become carriers), others have serious symptoms that include devastating diarrhea, and the treatment is nearly as unpleasant. The reason giardiasis has become "epidemic" is that there are more people in the backcountry—more people drinking water contaminated by animals—more people contaminating the water.

Whenever in doubt, boil the water 10 minutes. Keep in mind that *Giardia* can survive in water at or near freezing for weeks or months—a snow pond is not necessarily safe. Boiling is 100 percent effective against not only *Giardia* but the myriad other filthy little blighters (including those being brought home to America by returning jet-trekkers) that may upset your digestion or—as with some forms of hepatitis—destroy your liver.

If you cannot boil, use one of the several iodine treatments (chlorine compounds have been found untrustworthy in wildland circumstances) carried by mountain equipment shops. Rumor to the contrary, iodine treatments in the specified dosages pose no threat to the health of pregnant women or anyone else.

Some fancy-dancy patented devices sold in backpacking shops very well

Glacier-polished rocks at Spade Lake (Hike 69); for an air view, see photo on page 170.

serve certain purposes, such as filtering silt from the Ganges, but the price is high and the claims made for them often are so poorly documented that filtering always should be followed by the usual boiling or iodine treatment.

Litter and Garbage and Sanitation

It is rotten wildland manners to leave litter for others to worry about. The rule among considerate hikers is: if you can carry it in full, you can carry it out empty. Thanks to a steady improvement in manners, and the posting of wilderness rangers who glory in the name of garbage-collectors, American trails are cleaner than they have been since Columbus landed. Every hiker should learn to be a happy collector. On a day hike, take back to the road (and garbage can) every last orange peel and gum wrapper. On an overnight or longer hike, burn all paper (if a fire is built) but carry back all unburnables, including cans, metal foil, plastic, glass, and papers that won't burn.

Don't bury garbage. If fresh, animals will dig it up and scatter the remnants. Burning before burying is no answer either. Tin cans take as long as 40 years to disintegrate completely; aluminum and glass last for centuries. Furthermore, digging pits to bury junk disturbs the ground cover, and iron eventually leaches from buried cans and "rusts" springs and creeks.

Don't leave leftover food for the next travelers; they will have their own supplies and won't be tempted by such "gifts" spoiled by time or chewed by animals.

Especially don't cache plastic tarps. Weathering quickly ruins the fabric, little creatures nibble, and the result is a useless, miserable mess.

Keep the water pure. Don't wash dishes in streams or lakes, loosing food particles and detergent. Haul buckets of water off to the woods or rocks, and wash and rinse there. Eliminate body wastes in places well removed from watercourses; first dig a shallow hole in the "biological disposer layer," then touch a match to the toilet paper, which otherwise will be dug up by nosy critters and scattered about. (Better, use leaves.) Finally, cover the evidence. So managed, wastes are consumed in a matter of days. However, in heavy-use meadows the "biological disposer layer" may be full up. Increasingly it is advised to place the wastes in double, heavy-duty plastic bags and carry the evidence out of the wilderness.

Size

One management technique used to minimize impact in popular areas is to limit the number of people in any one group to a dozen or fewer. Hikers with very large families (or outing groups from clubs or wherever) should check the rules when planning a trip.

Lake Dorothy from Bear Lake trail (Hike 2)

Pets

Pets always have been forbidden on national park trails and now some parts of wildernesses are being closed.

Where pets are permitted, even a well-behaved dog can ruin someone else's trip. Some dogs noisily defend an ill-defined territory for their master, "guard" him on the trail, snitch enemy bacon, and are quite likely to defecate on the flat bit of ground the next hiker will want to sleep on. For a long time to come there will be plenty of "empty" country for those who hunt upland game with dogs or who simply can't enjoy a family outing without ol' Rover. However, the family that wants to go where the crowds are must leave its best friend home.

Do not depend on friendly tolerance of wilderness neighbors. Some people are so harassed at home by loose dogs that a hound in the wilderness has the same effect on them as a motorcycle. They may holler at you and turn you in to the ranger.

Dogs belong to the same family as coyotes, and even if no wildlife is visible, a dog's presence is sensed by the small wild things into whose home it is intruding.

Horses

As backcountry population grows the trend is toward designating certain trails and camps "Hiker Only," because some ecosystems cannot withstand the impact of large animals and some trails are not safe for them. However, many wilderness trails will continue to be "Hiker and Horse" (no motorcycles, no "mountain bikes") and the two must get along.

Most horse-riders do their best to be good neighbors on the trail and know how to go about it. The typical hiker, though, is ignorant of the difficulties inherent in maneuvering a huge mass of flesh (containing a very small brain) along narrow paths on steep mountains.

The first rule is: The horse has the *right of way*. For his own safety as well as that of the rider, the hiker must get off the trail—on the downhill side, preferably, giving the clumsy animal and its perilously perched rider the inside of the tread. The second rule is, when you see the horse approaching, do not keep silent or stand still in a mistaken attempt to avoid frightening the beast. Continue normal motions and speak to it, so the creature will recognize you as just another human and not think you a silent and doubtless dangerous monster.

Finally, if you have a dog along, get a tight grip on its throat to stop the nipping and yapping, which may endanger the rider and, in the case of a surly horse, the dog as well.

Theft

Equipment has become so fancy and expensive, so much worth stealing, and hikers so numerous, their throngs creating large assemblages of valuables, that theft is a growing problem. Not even wilderness camps are entirely safe, but the professionals who do most of the stealing mainly concentrate on cars. Rangers have the following recommendations.

First and foremost, don't make crime profitable. If the professionals break into a hundred cars and get nothing but moldy boots and tattered T-shirts they'll give up. The best bet is to arrive in a beat-up 1960 car with doors and windows that don't close and leave in it nothing of value. If you insist on driving a nice new car, at least don't have mag wheels, tape deck, and radio, and keep it empty of gear. Don't think locks help—pros can open your car door and trunk as fast with a picklock as you can with your key. Don't imagine you can hide anything from them—they know all the hiding spots. If the hike is part of an extended car trip, arrange to store your extra equipment at a nearby motel.

Be suspicious of anyone waiting at a trailhead. One of the tricks of the trade is to sit there with a pack as if waiting for a ride, watching new arrivals unpack—and hide their valuables—and maybe even striking up a conversation to determine how long the marks will be away.

The ultimate solution, of course, is for hikers to become as poor as they were in the olden days. No criminal would consider trailheads profitable if the loot consisted solely of shabby khaki war surplus.

Safety Considerations

The reason the Ten Essentials are advised is that hiking in the backcountry entails unavoidable risk that every hiker assumes and must be aware of and respect. The fact that a trail is described in this book is not a representation that it will be safe for you. Trails vary greatly in difficulty and in the degree of conditioning and agility one needs to enjoy them safely. On some hikes routes may have changed or conditions may have deteriorated since the descriptions were written. Also, trail conditions can change even from day to day owing to weather and other factors. A trail that is safe on a dry day or for a highly conditioned, agile, properly equipped hiker may be completely unsafe for someone else or unsafe under adverse weather conditions.

You can minimize your risks on the trail by being knowledgeable, prepared, and alert. There is not space in this book for a general treatise on safety in the mountains, but there are a number of good books and public courses on the subject and you should take advantage of them to increase your knowledge. Just as important, you should always be aware of your own limitations and of conditions existing when and where you are hiking. If conditions are dangerous, or if you are not prepared to deal with them safely, choose a different hike! It's better to have a wasted drive than to be the subject of a mountain rescue.

These warnings are not intended to scare you off the trails. Hundreds of thousands of people have safe and enjoyable hikes every year. However, one element of the beauty, freedom, and excitement of the wilderness is the presence of risks that do not confront us at home. When you hike you assume those risks. They can be met safely but only if you exercise your own independent judgment and common sense.

To help hikers have a safe and enjoyable trail experience by matching the trip to experience and physical condition, the Forest Service has begun signing trails as follows:

Requires limited skill and has little physical challenge. Tread is smooth, level, and wide, with generous clearing of trees, limbs, and other vegetation above and to each side of the trail to permit easy passage. Elevation gain or loss is minimal. Streams are most often crossed with bridges.

Requires a moderate skill level and provides a moderate physical challenge. Tread surface contains roots and embedded rocks. Clearing of trees, limbs, and other vegetation above and to each side of the trail results in occasional contact by the users. Elevation gain or loss is moderate. Streams are most often crossed by fords.

Requires a high degree of skill and provides a lot of physical challenge. Tread is seldom graded except on steep slopes for safety and prevention of soil erosion. Minimal clearing of trees, limbs, and other vegetation results in hampering the progress of the user. Elevation gain or loss is usually severe. Streams are crossed by fording and are sometimes difficult.

This rating system is good for comparing one trail to another. However, the actual difficulty encountered by a hiker will vary with the time of year, weather conditions, and the individual's physical ability.

Bridal Veil Falls on trail to Lake Serene

LAKE SERENE

Map: USGS Index

Since 1982 we have honored the request of Forest Service personnel that we not give directions on how to find the old trail to Lake Serene, which the Forest Service now considers dangerous. Even without directions, the trail is used by hundreds of hikers who climb the slippery rocks to the lake.

After 10 years of procrastination and problems obtaining easements on private land, the trail is now firmly scheduled and budgeted for construction in 1995. It will climb some 1800 feet in about 3 miles.

Workers will be blasting and rolling rocks. To facilitate the construction and for your own safety, stay off the trail until it is officially open. For current information contact the Skykomish Ranger Station.

Across-valley view of Mt. Index. Lake Serene is in the bowl at the base of the cliffs, Bridal Veil Falls below.

2 DOROTHY, BEAR, DEER, AND SNOQUALMIE LAKES

Round trip to Lake Dorothy from
  Miller River road 3 miles
Hiking time 2 hours
High point 3058 feet
Elevation gain 858 feet
Hikable June through mid-
  October
One day or backpack
Round trip to Snoqualmie Lake
  from Taylor River road 14½
  miles

Hiking time 8 hours
High point 3147 feet
Elevation gain 2000 feet
Hikable June through mid-
  October
One day or backpack
Map: Green Trails No. 175
  Skykomish
Current information: Ask at
  Skykomish Ranger Station
  about trail Nos. 1002 and 1072

Lying in a string on both sides of the Snoqualmie–Skykomish divide, these four large subalpine lakes once were so remote that only the sturdiest Scouts and fishermen could visit on a weekend; the usual trip was a week. Then logging roads pushed so far up the valleys that Dorothy was a mere 1½ miles from the car and Snoqualmie 2¼ miles—and there even were plans for a "Lake Dorothy Highway" that would have skirted all the shores! But as the wilderness concept gained strength a new attitude developed toward roads, not every one of which was considered permanently sacred. Logging roads were permitted to dwindle to footroads, transitional to trails, making the four lakes much lonesomer. However, renewed timber sales reopened the road on the Miller River side, so Lake Dorothy is once again the hangout of weekend rowdies with their beer busts, and the same fate may await the Taylor River road and Snoqualmie Lake. For now, though, the latter is decently remote and considerable solitude is possible for campers at the two middle lakes, Bear and Deer.

Drive US 2 east 17.5 miles from Gold Bar and just before the highway

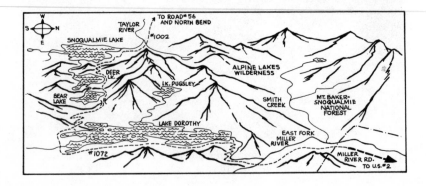

Snoqualmie Lake

tunnel turn right, at a sign for Money Creek Campground, on Old Cascade Highway. At a Y in 1.2 miles turn right onto gravel Miller River road and drive 8.3 miles to the trailhead, 2200 feet.

The trail climbs through forest to Lake Dorothy at 1½ miles, 3058 feet. It follows the east side of the 2-mile-long lake, crosses the marshy inlet, begins climbing, and at 4½ miles from the road tops the 3800-foot ridge dividing the Miller and Taylor Rivers. Views are down to island-dotted Dorothy amid forest and gray-white cliffs and southeast to the dominant peak of the area, 6670-foot Big Snow Mountain.

From the pass the way is downhill to Bear Lake, 3610 feet, and, at 6 miles, Deer Lake, 3583 feet. At 6½ miles is Snoqualmie Lake, 3147 feet, second-largest of the group. The trail continues 2¼ miles down the Taylor River to the end of a closed-off logging road become pleasant footroad, elevation 1865 feet (Hike 92). Amble on down a scant 6 miles, pausing to admire a series of spectacular granite-slab waterfalls, to the parking area at 1225 feet.

To protect vegetation, campers are asked to use designated sites.

View southeast from Tonga Ridge

SKYKOMISH RIVER
Alpine Lakes Wilderness

3 TONGA RIDGE–FISHER LAKE

Round trip to Sawyer Pass 6½ miles
Hiking time 3 hours
High point 4800 feet
Elevation gain 400 feet
Hikable July through October
One day or backpack
Round trip to Fisher Lake 9½ miles
Hiking time 4 hours
High point 5160 feet

Elevation gain 760 feet in, 397 feet out
Hikable mid-July through mid-October
One day or backpack
Maps: Green Trails No. 175 Skykomish and No. 176 Stevens Pass
Current information: Ask at Skykomish Ranger Sation about trail No. 1058

The easiest ridge walk, and maybe the most popular, on the west side of the Cascades, the views grand, the meadows beautiful, and the entire summer full of flowers. Fisher Lake and Ptarmigan Lakes lie near the thronged gardens of Tonga Ridge but are secluded from the mainstream of foot traffic in quiet cirques. Fisherpeople feet originally beat out the route, and some stretches retain their shortest-distance-to-the-fish-is-a-straight-line style.

Drive US 2 east from Skykomish 1.8 miles and turn right on Foss River road No. 68. At 1.2 miles keep right on the main road. At 2.5 miles, pass under a railroad bridge. At 3.6 miles turn left on Tonga Ridge road No.

6830. At 7 miles turn right on road No. (6830)310 and continue 1.5 miles to the road-end, elevation 4300 feet.

The hike begins on an old fire trail climbing to the ridge crest. In a couple hundred feet, the foot trail turns off the fire trail into forest, winds through woods a while, and then follows the ridge top in meadows. At about 1½ miles the trail leaves the crest to contour around Mt. Sawyer, finally dropping a bit to Sawyer Pass, 3 miles, 4800 feet, dividing the drainages of Burn Creek and Fisher Creek. Good campsites, and also the first water of the trip, in the gentle swale of the pass, a large green meadow (commonly called N.P. Camp) that turns a brilliant red in fall.

For a wide-view sidetrip, scramble up 5501-foot Mt. Sawyer, the second large hill seen from the Tonga River approach. Leave the trail wherever the slopes look appealing and plow upward through the huckleberry bushes, gaining 700 feet. Try it in late August and eat your way through delicious fruit. The summit panorama includes Mt. Rainier, Hinman, Daniel, and more.

For Fisher Lake, at the upper end of Sawyer Pass take an unmarked right, for about 300 feet, then go left on the unsigned Fisher Lake trail, headed south. Beyond the saddle ascend a steep hill, cross a little creek back and forth, level for a brief breather at a small marsh, and climb a second hill. While wandering with the trail through a green acre of meadow, note two nameless ponds to the left.

Atop a third and final hill, 5160 feet, the trail splits. Turn left and drop a final ½ mile to Fisher Lake, 4763 feet.

Hikers with a bit of extra time and a good bloodhound sense may continue ½ mile across the Fisher Lake outlet and along faint tread to the two Ptarmigan Lakes. The path meanders this way and that and several times divides. Just before a steep gully dropping to the first lake, veer right beneath cliffs to a rockslide and follow it down to the shore, 4475 feet. Views up to Terrace Mountain, but no camps. Traverse south near the water on a field of boulders and at the far end find a path climbing to the second lake, 4559 feet, and a small campsite.

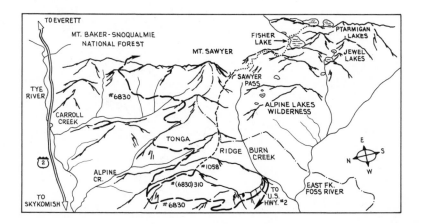

4 NECKLACE VALLEY

Round trip to Jade Lake 16 miles
Allow 2–3 days
High point 4600 feet
Elevation gain 3000 feet
Hikable late July through October

Maps: Green Trails No. 175 Skykomish and No. 176 Stevens Pass
Current information: Ask at Skykomish Ranger Station about trail No. 1062

A narrow alpine valley carved from the side of Mt. Hinman and appropriately named for its string of small gems—Jade, Emerald, and Opal Lakes. Nearby are Locket and Jewel Lakes. And others. Thanks to the long and at times very steep and rocky trail, this is much more lonesome country than the Foss Lakes area described in Hike 5.

Drive US 2 east from Skykomish 1.8 miles and turn right on Foss River road No. 68. At 3.6 miles pass the Tonga Ridge junction (Hike 3), and continue to the East Fork Foss River trail at 4.2 miles. On the left side of the road, find a parking area and the trailhead, elevation 1600 feet.

The first 5 miles gain only 600 feet and are very pleasant going through forest, following the valley bottom, passing the marshes of Alturas "Lake." The trail this far is very worthwhile in its own right and can be hiked on a day walk or a weekend backpack in May and June, when the high country is buried in snow.

The trail crosses a log over the river, which flows from the Hinman Glacier on Mt. Hinman and the Lynch Glacier on Mt. Daniel. On the far bank the trail leaves the river and begins a grueling climb into the hanging glacial trough, gaining 2400 feet in the 3 miles to the first gem of the necklace, Jade Lake, 4600 feet.

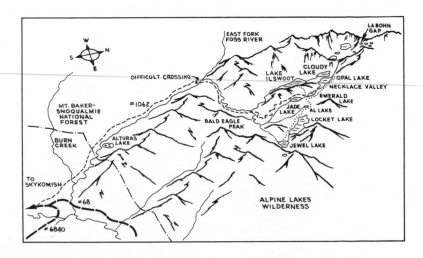

Necklace Valley and LaBohn Gap

Necklace Valley is a delightful mixture of forest, heather, ice-polished granite—and of course, lakes. Possibilities for roaming are endless. Campsites are available along the river and at most of the lakes; the best are at Emerald Lake.

From Emerald Lake, about ¼ mile upvalley from Jade Lake, cross a low saddle west to Jewel and Locket Lakes or cross the ridge east to Lake Ilswoot.

From the east side of Opal Lake, another ¼ mile upvalley from Emerald Lake, climb a short step up a tributary creek to Cloudy Lake.

Tough to attain are La Bohn Lakes, set in granite bowls near the summit of 5000-foot La Bohn Gap. The off-trail route from the head of Necklace Valley goes abruptly up through cliffs; no route can be recommended for any but experienced mountain travelers.

To preserve vegetation, campers are asked to use established sites only. Jade Lake is the most crowded; Ilswoot and Locket are quieter. Carry a stove; firewood is extremely scarce.

5 FOSS LAKES

**Round trip to Copper Lake
8 miles
Hiking time 6–8 hours
High point 3961 feet
Elevation gain 2300 feet
Hikable July through October
One day or backpack**

**Maps: Green Trails No. 175
Skykomish and No. 176 Stevens
Pass
Current information: Ask at
Skykomish Ranger Station about
trail No. 1064**

Lovers of alpine lakes look at the topo map and drool. Crowded onto a single sheet are 10 large lakes and numerous small ones, the rich legacy of ancient glaciers. The West Fork Foss River trail passes four of the lakes and fishermen's paths lead to others. Don't expect privacy—the area has long been famous and extremely popular for its numerous, unusually big, and readily accessible lakes.

Drive US 2 east from Skykomish 1.8 miles and turn right on Foss River road No. 68 for 4.2 miles to the East Fork Foss River trail (Hike 4), and continue to West Fork Foss River road No. 6835 (may be shown as No. 6840 on some maps). Turn left 2 miles to the road-end and trailhead, elevation 1600 feet.

Hike an easy 1½ miles in cool forest to the first of the chain, Trout Lake, 2000 feet. Trees line the shore; through branches are glimpses of rugged cliffs above. This far makes a leisurely afternoon; the trail is free of snow in May. On August 17, 1991, a storm triggered a giant rockslide that came within 100 feet of campers at Trout Lake, damming the outlet and raising the lake level 10 feet. Some forest campsites are now lakeside camps.

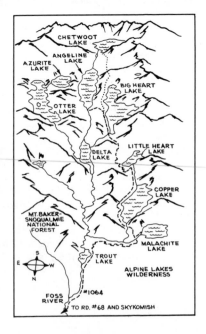

The steep, hot, 2-mile climb to Copper Lake, gaining 2000 feet, is something else in late summer. Water is plentiful but always out of reach—splashing in falls on the far hillside, rushing along a deep gully below the trail. The way at last opens into the cliff-walled basin of 3961-foot Copper Lake, surrounded by alpine trees and meadows and talus slopes.

Though much can be seen in a day or weekend, 3 days or more are needed for a satisfying exploration. Copper Lake marks the beginning of highland terrain, of glacier-smoothed rock knolls and granite

Rock avalanche that swept across the trail on August 17, 1991

buttresses and miles of heather and blueberries amid groves of alpine trees. The crowds steadily diminish beyond Copper.

The lovely cirque of Malachite Lake, 4089 feet, is reached by a steep ¼-mile path branching from the main trail ½ mile before Copper Lake.

Beyond Copper Lake the main trail climbs gently along a stream, passing the best and maybe the only flower display of the trip, to 4204-foot Little Heart Lake, 1 mile from Copper, then crosses a 4700-foot ridge and drops to 4545-foot Big Heart Lake, 2½ miles from Copper; during the ridge crossing take a short sidetrip from the trail for an overlook of three lakes.

The formal trail continues beyond the outlet of Big Heart Lake 1 mile, over the end of the ridge, to the outlet of 4609-foot Angeline Lake. Chetwoot Lake, 4905 feet, coldest and rockiest of the group, may be reached by leaving the formal trail at about its high point on the ridge and traveling south over the very summit of the high and narrow ridge between Big Heart and Angeline Lakes, down into a saddle, and up once more over the next ridge. The route is a bit rugged but quite feasible, a footpath beaten much of the way. From Chetwoot the upper end of Angeline Lake is readily accessible.

There are also Delta, Azurite, and Otter Lakes and a dozen or more smaller ones, many visible from the trail and each a jewel in its own right. Boot-beaten tracks exist to all of them but essentially they are for the experienced cross-country hiker.

All camps at all the lakes are heavily used and usually crowded. Carry a stove if you want hot food or boiled drinking water. To preserve vegetation, use established sites only. At Trout Lake only designated sites may be used. Camping is very limited at Malachite, Little Heart, and Chetwoot Lakes and virtually impossible at Angeline. Copper has a large expanse of people-beaten dirt. The most scenic camping is at Big Heart.

6 DECEPTION CREEK

Round trip to campsite 6 miles
Hiking time 4 hours
High point 3200 feet
Elevation gain 1400 feet
Hikable June through October
One day or backpack

Map: Green Trails No. 176 Stevens
** Pass**
Current information: Ask at
** Skykomish Ranger Station**
** about trail No. 1059**
Note: In 1992 floods, the foot-
bridges were lost.

For quick routes to lakes and views and meadows, and for easy valley-bottom strolls, go elsewhere in the Alpine Lakes Wilderness. However, for deep immersion in virgin forest and close encounters with a splendid white brawl of water, Deception Creek is the place. The trail makes an excellent exit for a loop hike, as well as a superb late-spring and early-summer walk when the high country remains monotonously wintry. Enjoy the boulders draped in licorice fern, the walls dripping delicate maidenhair fern, the bogs of wicked-looking devils club, and the blossoms of queens cup and Canadian dogwood bursting from the moss-covered forest floor.

Drive US 2 east 8 miles from Skykomish, to 0.2 mile beyond the Deception Falls parking area, and immediately turn right on road No. 6088, signed "Deception Creek Trail" (unsigned in 1991). In 0.4 mile pass beneath a railroad trestle to the road-end and trailhead, elevation 2000 feet.

Trail No. 1059 parallels Deception Creek a scant ½ mile, crosses the creek at the wilderness boundary, and that's the end of easy strolling. The way gains 1000 feet to get above wooded cliffs and at 2 miles crosses Sawyer Creek. From its 3200-foot high point at 2½ miles, the trail drops 200 feet to a delightful campsite beside Deception Creek, 2800 feet, a good turnabout.

The trail crosses the creek on a log and in the next 2 miles has another crossing, numerous ups and downs, and passes several lonesome camps. At 5 miles is a junction with a trail from a nearby road on Tonga Ridge (Hike 3), formerly an obnoxious shortcut entry but now in the process of

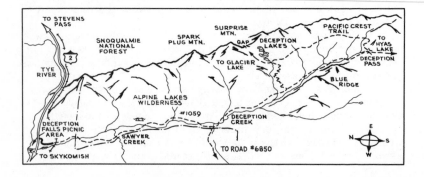

Second crossing of Deception Creek

gradual obliteration. At 7½ miles is a junction with the Deception Lakes trail. At 10½ miles the path joins the Pacific Crest Trail at Deception Pass; any number of loops and one-way trips may be hooked into here.

Mount Daniel from Surprise Gap

SKYKOMISH RIVER
Alpine Lakes Wilderness

7   SURPRISE LAKE AND DECEPTION LAKES

Round trip to Surprise Lake 8½ miles
Hiking time 5 hours
High point 4508 feet
Elevation gain 2300 feet
Hikable late June through October
One day or backpack
Round trip to Deception Lakes 19½ miles

Allow 2 days
High point 5900 feet
Elevation gain 3700 feet in, 850 feet out
Hikable late July through October
Map: Green Trails No. 176 Stevens Pass
Current information: Ask at Skykomish Ranger Station about trail No. 1060

Surprise Lake mirrors a ring of green trees and white granite. Glacier Lake adds the cliffs of Surprise Mountain, whose summit is the supreme grandstand for viewing the glacial brilliance of Daniel and Hinman, forest deeps of Deception Creek, and peaks from Baring to Monte Cristo to Glacier to Cashmere.

Drive US 2 east from Skykomish 10 miles to the hamlet of Scenic, service center for the Burlington-Northern Railroad's Cascade Tunnel, whose west portal is nearby. Just before the highway overpass above the railroad tracks, go right on an unsigned road. Drive over the railroad tracks, and in a hundred feet turn right 0.1 mile on a sideroad with a hiker-trail symbol and park, elevation 2200 feet.

Walk the abandoned road ¼ mile, following the powerline swath to the beginning of Surprise Creek trail No. 1060, which quickly leaves hot brush for cool trees. No other hike in the vicinity offers a more joyful forest, so many excellent waterfalls, and exactly the proper trickles and gushes to splash face and head (despite green shadows, these can become quite dry, particularly on switchbacks of the final mile, where the trail parallels a continuous cataract up into the hanging valley). At 4 miles pass the Trap Pass trail, in a few more feet cross Surprise Creek amongst a confusion of trails, and reach Surprise Lake, 4508 feet. A picnic lunch atop a granite buttress climaxes a nice day.

On the way to Deception Lakes, the trail avoids Glacier Lake, 4806 feet, but sidepaths give easy access. At ¾ mile from the Surprise outlet, the trail joins the Pacific Crest Trail near the 5100-foot base of Surprise Mountain's 1000-foot walls.

The Crest Trail turns right and climbs to 5900-foot Pieper Pass, the way to Deception Lakes and points south, as well as takeoff for off-trail explorations to Spark Plug Mountain and Spark Plug Lake. At 9¾ miles from the road, the trail reaches Deception Lakes, 5053 feet, amid miles of parkland and meadows and marmots.

For the big picture find the old fire-lookout trail to the summit of Surprise Mountain, 6330 feet. Naught remains of the lookout cabin except a litter of fragments—and the metal post that was the base of the firefinder. The views! Precipitously down spectacular cliffs to the lakes. Across the broad valley to the gleaming ice. West to saltwater, north to volcanoes, east to Enchantments.

Camps are numerous at and near both lakes and at the site of the old shelter cabin. Wood is scarce at best; carry a stove. To preserve vegetation, campers are asked to shun the shores. Carry water and camp near the summit of Surprise and see more stars than are dreamt of in your astronomy charts.

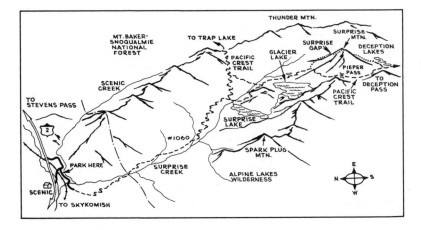

8 HOPE LAKE AND MIG LAKE

Round trip to Mig Lake 4 miles
Hiking time 3 hours
High point 4650 feet
Elevation gain 1650 feet
Hikable mid-July through
    September
One day or backpack
Map: Green Trails No. 176
    Stevens Pass
Current information: Ask at
    Skykomish Ranger Station
    about trail No. 1061

Fields of heather and blueberries and clumps of sturdy subalpine trees ring two alpine lakes. Though small by Alpine Lakes Wilderness standards, Hope and Mig offer pleasant camping and are excellently located for exploring the Pacific Crest Trail north toward Stevens Pass and south to Trap Lake.

Drive US 2 east from Skykomish 12 miles, cross Tunnel Creek bridge, and just before the highway widens to four lanes go right on road No. 6095 (only possible from the eastbound lane). At 0.6 mile the road forks; go right on road No. (6095)110, crossing a cement bridge. At

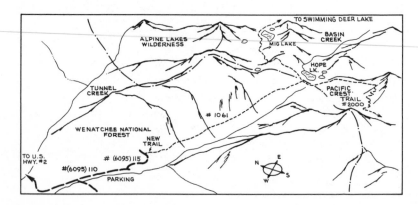

Cotton grass at Mig Lake

0.8 mile, the next junction, go straight ahead, avoiding a second bridge. At 1.2 miles the road splits again. Go left, steeply up on road No. (6095)115, and at 1.3 miles find Tunnel Creek trailhead No. 1061, elevation 3000 feet.

Ascend the valley in cool green forest on tread kept in superb condition by adopt-a-trail volunteers of The Mountaineers. The way is steep and never in sight of Tunnel Creek until the final ¼ mile. At 1½ miles is Hope Lake, 4400 feet; the large campsites are definite invitations to spend time exploring.

From Hope Lake turn left on Interstate 2000 (the Pacific Crest Trail) ½ mile to Mig Lake, 4650 feet, and more camps.

These two are only the beginning of the lakes. North 2 miles from Mig Lake is Swimming Deer Lake (Hike 9). Josephine and Susan Jane are a bit beyond. South from Hope 3 miles along a scenic ridge are the rock-bound shores of Trap Lake.

9   SWIMMING DEER LAKE

Round trip to Swimming Deer Lake 10 miles
Hiking time 8 hours
High point 5200 feet
Elevation gain 1600 feet in, 1000 feet out
Hikable mid-July through mid-October

One day or backpack
Map: Green Trails No. 176 Stevens Pass
Current information: Ask at Skykomish Ranger Station about trail No. 2000

A person's fondest recollections of this stretch of the Cascade Crest may well be not of hiking in sunshine but in a fog or slow-drifting clouds, when distant views do not compete with foreground miniatures of heather and blueberries and Christmas trees, and when mists hide until the last mo-

Josephine Lake

ment surprises around turns in the trail—little marshes and ponds, flower-rimmed meadow lakelets, bigger lakes in rock-walled cirques, and perhaps a swimming deer.

Drive US 2 to Stevens Pass, and just east of the Forest Service residence on the south side of the highway turn into the large parking lot, elevation 4061 feet.

Though the Pacific Crest Trail sets out up ski slopes, it is plainly and solidly built, ascending steadily in trees and rockslides to the Cascade Crest at 1½ miles, 5150 feet. It then descends ¼ mile to a powerline swath and service road, the route to undisturbed terrain clearly delineated by markers. The trail traverses patches of forest, wet meadows rich in flower color, and open talus with views out Mill Creek to the Nason Creek valley and Nason Ridge. At 3¼ miles en-

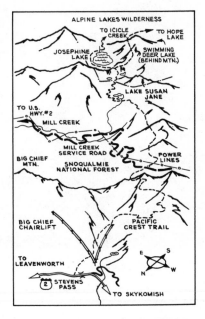

ter Alpine Lakes Wilderness. At 3½ miles is Lake Susan Jane, 4595 feet, a modest tarn tucked in a tiny cirque, cliffs above, valley below. Here are the first camps, quite pleasant, if heavily pounded.

Shift down to climb through meadows by ponds to a 4950-foot saddle. Just beyond, at 4 miles, 5000 feet, is a junction with Icicle Creek trail No. 1551. This is the route to Chain Lakes (Hike 10) and also, immediately below, Josephine Lake, 4681 feet, large and rocky and forest-shored; campsites near the outlet.

Enjoy the views down to the blue lakes and out to the Stuart Range and continue south on the Crest Trail, climbing heather fields to round the corner of another open ridge at 5200 feet. In 1 mile from the junction find a sidetrail down to the broad parkland bench, 4681 feet, where the shores of Swimming Deer Lake wind in and out of clumps of subalpine trees, and camps on wooded knolls suggest stopping over a night or two for explorations.

If pickup transportation can be arranged, a one-way hike can be made south on the Crest Trail, exiting via Tunnel Creek (Hike 8) or Surprise Creek (Hike 7).

Upper Doelle Lake

SKYKOMISH RIVER
Alpine Lakes Wilderness

ᏚᎾ CHAIN LAKES–DOELLE LAKES

**Round trip to Chain Lakes
22 miles
Allow 3–4 days
High point 5700 feet
Elevation gain 3600 feet in, 1600
feet out
Hikable late July through
September**

**Maps: Green Trails No. 176 Stevens
Pass and No. 177 Chiwaukum
Mountains
Current information: Ask at
Leavenworth Ranger Station
about trail Nos. 1551, 1569, and
2000**

The most spectacular peak in this corner of the Cascades is the 6807-foot fang of Bulls Tooth, highest of a mile-long line of granite splinters and blocks. Beneath the ridge's cliffs on one side lie the two Doelle Lakes in twin cirques scooped from the granite, and beneath it on the other, in a mile-long glacial trough, lie the three Chain Lakes, so deeply shadowed that snow lasts late and comes early and the trees grow few and small in arctic meadowlands. If these aren't attractions enough, the spot is among the lonesomest in the Alpine Lakes Wilderness because no matter which approach is chosen the miles are many and the elevation gain much; the access described here is about as easy as the trip can be done.

Hike the Pacific Crest Trail 4 miles from Stevens Pass to a junction,

4960 feet, with Icicle Creek trail No. 1551 (Hike 9). Follow it left and down, past campsites at Josephine Lake, 4681 feet, and more near the junction with Whitepine Creek trail (Hike 11), an alternate entry route. At 3½ miles from the Crest Trail, reach the junction with Chain Lakes trail No. 1569, 3800 feet. This is at a point on the Icicle Creek trail 8½ miles from the Icicle road, another and somewhat easier alternate entry (Hike 28).

The ascent of Chain Creek valley begins with a dizzying series of short switchbacks in forest, concludes with a steady sidehill climb in trees and openings that give looks out over Icicle country. At 2½ miles, 5628 feet, hard labor abruptly ceases at the lip of the hanging trough and shores of the first lake, long and narrow and rocky. As it ends the second lake begins, the valley broadening out in parkland and meadow. Cross the outlet of the second lake, go left, by a string of ponds and jumbles of giant granite blocks, around the corner of a delightful knoll, and at 11 miles from Stevens Pass come to the final and most magical lake, 5690 feet, amid a broad flat of grass and flowers meandered by cold little creeks from snowfields on slopes of the crags.

As worries mount over human pressures in fragile wildlands, here is an example of what can be done by sensitive management and respectful users. When first described in this guidebook, the basin was a squalor of garbage and dung. Wilderness rangers have cleaned up the mess and all but a few horsemen and hikers have cleaned up their acts.

Scenic camps (no fires, carry a stove) can be found, bases for clambering the ridges and exploring nooks. To start, from the junction at the second lake go left, then left again before the third lake to take the 1-mile trail steeply up talus to a 6200-foot notch in Bulls Tooth Ridge and steeply down heather gardens to Doelle Lakes, 5775 and 5635 feet, deep and cliff-walled.

Experienced wildland navigators may neatly exit—and make a loop— from Doelle Lakes by proceeding a short way down the abandoned Doughgod Creek trail and then up and down a meager but definite (if intermittent) track to Frosty Pass. Return to square one via Frosty Creek and Icicle Creek trails.

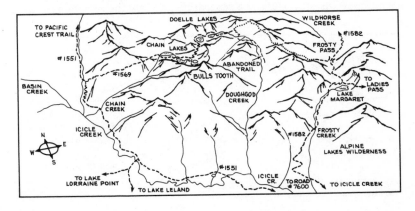

11 WHITEPINE CREEK

Round trip to Mule Creek Camp
12 miles
Hiking time 7 hours
High point 3600 feet
Elevation gain 800 feet
Hikable July through mid-
October
One day or backpack

Maps: Green Trails No.145
Wenatchee Lake, No. 176 Stevens
Pass, and No. 177 Chiwaukum
Mountains
Current information: Ask at
Wenatchee Lake Ranger Station
about trail No. 1582

Curious about what it was like to hike in the Cascades when your daddy was a boy? Here's a valley for getting the feel of the olden days, when trail crews came through only once in every so many years to chop the brush in avalanche swaths and saw through windfalls, when the horses of sheepherders and hunters churned every stretch of wet tread to a mudbath, and when to meet another human being was to be as startled as Robinson Crusoe was by Friday. Aside from the solitude there is quiet virgin forest. Lonesome camps are great places to sit around the fire listening to coyotes sing.

Drive US 2 east from Stevens Pass 14 miles, west from Coles Corner 6.6 miles, and turn off on the plainly signed, well-maintained Whitepine Road. Follow it 3.7 miles to the end and the Whitepine trailhead, elevation 2800 feet.

Trail No. 1582 begins in an old clearcut, quickly enters open forest, and commences a gradual ascent in sound and occasional sight of the creek; occasional avalanche swaths and cliff bands give views over the valley.

At 1 mile enter Alpine Lakes Wilderness and at 2½ miles come to the junction with the Wildhorse trail (Hike 12), 3200 feet. Just before the junction is a camp; another is a few feet up the right fork, beside Whitepine Creek, which a horse bridge used to cross before the floods of late 1990. Look around for a footlog crossing. Or wade. But not in snow-melt time! Since most traffic goes the Wildhorse way, to Frosty Pass, the Whitepine way now leaps the generation gap into the remote past. Be-

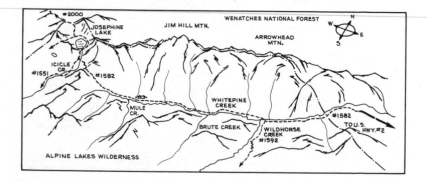

Tributary of Whitepine Creek

yond a small camp at the site of long-gone Arrowhead Guard Station, the trail alternates between forest and avalanche brush to a grassy little meadow at 6 miles, 3600 feet. Here, at the base of the old Mule Creek sheep driveway, is a good turnaround for a day or weekend hike.

To continue is to delve deeper into the past than some hikers might like, the brush denser and the mudholes deeper. From the camp the trail crosses a wide avalanche path terminating in the boulders and gravel and mud of a blowout flood. Clamber across and enter forest for the last time, climbing to the timbered saddle, 7³/₄ miles, 4640 feet, between Whitepine and Icicle Creek drainage. A final ¹/₂ mile drops to the Icicle trail, 4400 feet (Hikes 9 and 28).

12 WILDHORSE CREEK

Round trip to Frosty Pass 18½
  miles
Allow 3–4 days
High point 5700 feet
Elevation gain 2900 feet plus
  ups and downs
Hikable mid-July through
  September

Maps: Green Trails No. 145 Wenatchee
  Lake and No. 177 Chiwaukum
  Mountains
Current information: Ask at
  Wenatchee Lake Ranger Station
  about trail Nos. 1582 and 1592

How many years ago did the fire burn so hot as to incinerate the entire forest on both sides of the valley, from near the creek all the way up to the meadows? A century ago? Whenever, it was so long ago that there is no silver forest of standing snags, even the fallen logs are lines of rot, and the post-blaze trees scattered amid the huckleberry bushes and mountain misery and mountain ash are, though many decades old, scarcely more than shrubs. That is one of the trip's distinctions. Another is the fact that despite being wide-open to the sun the path is deliciously well watered by

Upper Wildhorse Creek valley

all-summer creeks tumbling from the snowfields, high above, on the mighty peaks of the Chiwaukum Mountains.

Drive to Whitepine Creek trailhead, elevation 2800 feet, and hike 2½ miles to the junction at 3200 feet (Hike 11).

Wildhorse trail No. 1592 instantly sets out escaping the trees, steeply in an alternation of shady forest and open avalanche paths, then steeply still in a series of switchbacks. Beyond the last of these, the way gradually emerges from forest to the naked slopes of brush and pioneering firs and pines. Between 4500 feet (4½ miles) and 4800 feet (5½ miles) are three small big-vista camps, beside or near fine splashing creeks. At the last of these, the path steeply ascends around a spur ridge to 5200 feet and commences a yo-yo traverse in continuous views over Wildhorse and Whitepine country to Jim Hill Mountain, Bulls Tooth, and Glacier Peak. Always close above are peaks of the Chiwaukums, culminating in many-summited Snowgrass Mountain.

Based at any of the camps, the canny wildlander may ascend burn meadow, then subalpine meadow, to the high views from Deadhorse Pass, 7200 feet, possibly on bits of the ancient path, or to snowfields in cozy pocket basins at the base of the crags. The most popular destinations are Grace Lakes (no fires, carry a stove), 6242 feet, attained via an abandoned but much-used trail that takes off at 8¼ miles.

At 8¾ miles is the last camp before the final climb to Frosty Pass, 5700 feet, 9¼ miles, and the junction with the Icicle Ridge trail (Hike 19). To the left ¾ mile are overcrowded camps at Lake Mary (Hike 33). To the right ¼ mile along the meadow saddle is Frosty Pass, from which Frosty Creek trail No. 1593 drops ¾ mile to Lake Margaret's small and overused camps. A sign at the pass, "Horse Camps," points the short distance to Table Camp, often deserted when Lake Mary is Tent City and offering long looks out the Wildhorse. The trail actually continues past the camp, eventually leading to Doelle Lakes (Hike 10), but only if you don't get lost, which is not too difficult.

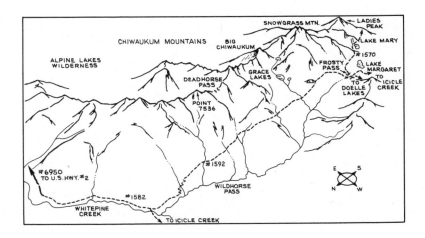

13 LAKE ETHEL

Round trip 9 miles
Hiking time 5 hours
High point 5700 feet
Elevation gain 3300 feet
Hikable mid-July through
September
One day or backpack

Maps: Green Trails No. 145
Wenatchee Lake and No. 177
Chiwaukum Mountains
Current information: Ask at
Wenatchee Lake Ranger Station
about trail No. 1585

Exactly where deep forest yields to steep green meadows at the north end of the Chiwaukum Mountains, Lake Ethel perches in its cirque, on the border of the wide-open roaming country. Getting there, though, is less than half the fun—three times the trail crosses a private (gated) logging road and is frequently in view of clearcuts extending to the boundary of the Alpine Lakes Wilderness, a few feet from the lake.

Drive US 2 east from Stevens Pass 16.3 miles to road No. 6940 on the southeast side of the highway. Cross Nason Creek and take the first left 0.2 mile, bumping over railroad tracks to a junction under the powerlines. Take the left, signed "Not Maintained for Passenger Cars," 0.2 teeth-rattling mile to a split. Stay left 0.2 mile to the next split; go right. The road returns to the powerlines, where most cars will plead to be parked, before dropping to ford a creek and rumble over several gravel bars. In 0.2 mile the road returns to forest for a final peaceful 0.2 mile to the trailhead at the first switchback, elevation 2400 feet.

The way begins on an old road that soon narrows to well-graded trail. Views are excellent over highway, airstrip, powerlines, and train tracks to the green upsweep of Nason Ridge. In 1½ steady-climbing miles, the trail attains a ridge above Gill Creek and stays there 2½ miles, in forest except where logged. Just before 2 miles is the first road (gated) crossing and shortly before 3 miles the last.

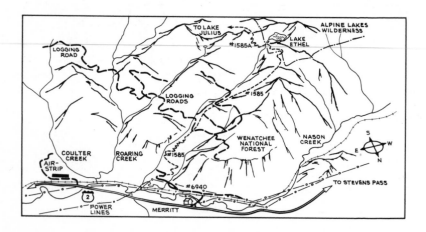

Nason Creek valley from Lake Ethel trail

At 3½ miles, 5700 feet, the trail abruptly turns left and drops from the ridge to Gill Creek, at 4¼ miles joining the old trail that followed Gill Creek—until the valley was clearcut by heirs of the Northern Pacific Land Grant. Go right ¼ mile to a junction with Upper Roaring Creek trail No. 1584, leading to Lake Julius and McCue Ridge (Hike 16). Continue straight ahead, entering Alpine Lakes Wilderness, to Lake Ethel, 5500 feet, and a large camping area.

Hikers with happy feet may follow the Upper Roaring Creek trail 1 mile to the open ridge between Gill Creek and Roaring Creek and 1½ more miles to fine views of Lake Julius, Lake Ethel, McCue Ridge, and especially the long rampart of the high and mighty Chiwaukum Mountains (Hike No.14).

Lake Julius

NASON CREEK
Partially in Alpine Lakes Wilderness

 14   SCOTTISH LAKES

Round trip to Loch Eileen from Chiwaukum Creek trailhead 29 miles
Allow 3 days
High point 5900 feet
Elevation gain 3400 feet in, 800 feet out
Hikable mid-July through mid-September

Maps: Green Trails No. 178 Leavenworth and No. 179 Chiwaukum
Current information: Ask at Wenatchee Lake Ranger Station about trail Nos. 1571, 1584B, 1585, and 1591

Some of the finest alpine highlands of the Alpine Lakes Wilderness, enclosing four lovely lakes. However, into every paradise a little horror must fall. Thanks to the 1864 railroad land grant, the forest trail up Roaring Creek has been obliterated and access to those jewels is through a private timber mine on logging roads. Of the three approaches only one, the longest, can be considered purely wild.

Lake Ethel approach: round trip 17 miles. Elevation gain 4000 feet. Only a short portion is in wilderness. Most of the way is within sight and sound of logging roads.

Scottish Lakes Nomad Camp: round trip 22 miles. Elevation gain 4000 feet. Approach is by a 9-mile (gated) road belonging to Longview Fiber Co. Scottish Lakes Nomad Camp (a primitive backcountry hotel served by private bus) is only 2 miles from the lakes. Call (509) 538-7330.

Chiwaukum Creek approach: described here is the longest but purest—well, almost; a short stretch is on private land, which is to say, a clearcut. The surviving public forest is magnificent, Chiwaukum Lake beautiful, and the views from McCue Ridge outstanding.

Drive to Chiwaukum Creek trailhead, elevation 1800 feet (Hike 15). Hike 9½ miles, rounding Chiwaukum Lake, 5200 feet, to the junction with McCue Ridge trail No. 1574. Go left, ascending well-graded trail 1½ miles to the crest of McCue Ridge, 5750 feet; for the views walk a few hundred feet east to a big patch of snowbrush and gaze over the vast Chiwaukum valley to the Chiwaukum Mountains, culminating in the 8000-foot peaks of Snowgrass, and to the Cashmere Crags of the Stuart Range.

The trail drops 250 feet from the crest to intersect Upper Roaring Creek trail No. 1574. Go left, descending open forest into Roaring Creek valley, cross the creek on a footlog, and at 14 miles, 5100 feet, go left on trail No. 1584B to Lake Julius, 5190 feet, 14½ miles from the road. The trail continues, climbing another 300 feet to Loch Eileen.

For explorations, scramble from the south shore of Loch Eileen up to Lake Donald, tucked beneath McCue Ridge, or roam the 7000-foot-plus summits of the Chiwaukum Mountains, discovering tiny cirques and hidden meadows.

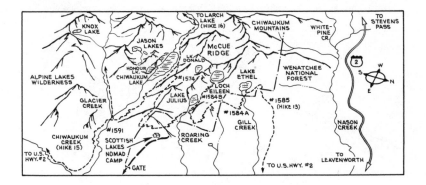

15   CHIWAUKUM CREEK

Round trip to Lake Flora 23 miles
Allow 3–4 days
High point 5700 feet
Elevation gain 3900 feet
Hikable mid-July through
  September

Maps: Green Trails No. 178
  Leavenworth and No. 177
  Chiwaukum Mountains
Current information: Ask at
  Leavenworth Ranger Station
  about trail No. 1571

The most popular route to meadow highlands of the exceedingly popular "Mormon Lakes" is from the other side of the mountain (Hike 33), which means the trail population is denser there and the camps more thronged. This route is longer and thus lonesomer.

Drive US 2 east 25.8 miles from Stevens Pass or west 1 mile from Tumwater Campground and turn south on Chiwaukum Creek road No. 7908 for 0.3 mile to the trailhead, elevation 1800 feet.

Hike the gated road past private homes 1½ miles to its end and the start of trail No. 1571. The way ascends imperceptibly, upsy-downsy, touching the stream at small camps. The forest in the narrow, steep-walled valley is deep-shadowed and big-tree and mossy and spring-oozy, the most enchanting woods walk in the vicinity and a joyous easy-afternoon stroll. The climax of such trips, the standard turnaround point, used to be at 4 miles in groves of giant ponderosa pines that sent tree-huggers into delirium. They therefore fought bitterly to prevent the loggers who had climbed the other side of McCue Ridge from descending here. They lost; the glory spot was placed in the Alpine Lakes Wilderness—but not until the groves had been butchered. It is some satisfaction that the conservationists' uproar caused the harvesting to be "selective" (selecting all the big trees) and the access road from the ridge to be put to bed (for cars, not for motorcycles, whose racket intrudes what is otherwise a wheel-free valley). Indeed, a hiker who fails to notice the stumps will suppose the for-

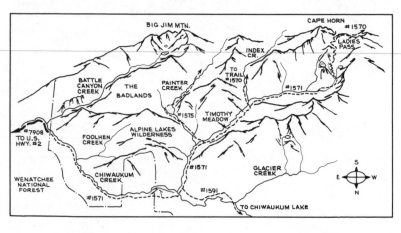

Grindstone Mountain from Ladies Pass

est to be virgin, if mediocre. Those who remember the ponderosas moan and scream the whole mile of stump-lined trail.

Virgin and superb forest is reentered. At 5½ miles, 3300 feet, creek and trail split. Shortly after crossing the stream on a cedar log, North Fork Chiwaukum trail No. 1591 goes right to Chiwaukum Lake (Hike 16). Stay left on trail No. 1571 along the South Fork.

The deep green slot of a valley opens to wider and airier dimensions, forest interspersed with rockslides and avalanche brush. At 7 miles, 3700 feet, is a pleasant, grassy camp by the junction with Painter Creek trail (Hike 18). The way climbs a valley step, passing a splendid falls where the creek tumbles over ledges of gaudy gneiss, and levels out to Timothy Meadow, 8 miles, 4000 feet, the tall grass and bright flowers ringed by shining-white aspen trees, a favorite campsite.

At 8½ miles, 4100 feet, is the overgrown junction with Index Creek trail. The valley head now can be seen, terminating abruptly in a steep-walled amphitheater from which escape seems impossible. The trail crosses the South Fork (easily, the stream now much reduced in size) at 10 miles and again at 10½ miles and then finds the magical escape, squirming up the headwall in short switchbacks and, at 11½ miles, 5700 feet, flattening out in heather meadows of Lake Flora. Just across a spur in a separate cirque is the patriarch of all these lovely lady lakes, Lake Brigham.

The South Fork trail dreamily roams a final mile upward in flowers to Ladies Pass, 6800 feet, and ends. But the trip has just begun, for here is the junction with Icicle Ridge trail (Hike 19); and the sky-surrounded tundras of Snowgrass Mountain await above.

16 CHIWAUKUM LAKE– LARCH LAKE

Round trip to Chiwaukum Lake
  19 miles
Allow 2–3 days
High point 5400 feet
Elevation gain 3600 feet
Hikable mid-July through mid-October
Round trip to Larch Lake
  20 miles
Allow 2–3 days
High point 6078 feet

Elevation gain 4178 feet
Hikable mid-July through mid-October
Maps: Green Trails No. 177 Chiwaukum Mountains and No. 178 Leavenworth
Current information: Ask at Leavenworth Ranger Station about trail Nos. 1571 and 1591

In the shadow of the tall, rugged Chiwaukum Mountains lie two lakes rimmed by rocks and groves of larch, basecamps for high wandering. As happy as the destination is, the approach is through lovely forest, by comfortable camps, with charming views of the stream, including a cascading waterfall just above one of three handsome bridges.

Drive to the Chiwaukum Creek trailhead, elevation 1800 feet (see Hike 15 for directions).

Walk trail No. 1571 to the forks of creek and trail at 5½ miles, 3300 feet. Go right on North Fork Chiwaukum trail No. 1591, climbing over a large terminal moraine of the ancient valley glacier, then winding around a large marsh, successor to the former moraine-dammed lake. At 7½ miles cross Glacier Creek to a sprawling horse camp, the turnaround for hooves; beyond here the valley is hiker-only. The valley head in view, the trail steeply and hotly ascends a 1200-foot step in the old glacial trough via a gigantic talus, the excellent views of valley and Chiwaukum Mountains good excuses for pausing to gasp and pant. At 9 miles, 5400 feet, the top of the step is attained and the way traverses ½ mile beneath rugged

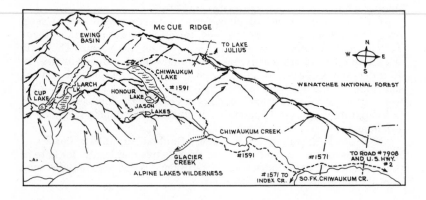

cliffs to Chiwaukum Lake, 9½ miles, 5210 feet.

The path follows the shore, passing campsites, ½ mile to a junction with McCue Ridge trail (Hike 14), and proceeds beyond the lake to more camps in Ewing Basin, a flat ½ mile long and ¼ mile wide. A way trail crosses the basin and a small creek and climbs steeply through forest and meadows to Larch Lake, 11½ miles, 6078 feet, and many good camps. To preserve vegetation, here and elsewhere, hikers are asked to use designated sites. No fires at Larch Lake; carry a stove or camp elsewhere.

Explorations abound. From Chiwaukum Lake cross the outlet to Honour Lake and scramble up the hill to Jason Lakes. From Larch Lake ascend gardens to tiny Cup Lake, set at 6443 feet in a north-facing cirquelet that doesn't melt free of snow until September, if then. Find an old way trail and continue to the crest of the Chiwaukum Mountains in the arctic-barren fellfields of 7200-foot Deadhorse Pass, overlooking Wildhorse and Whitepine Creeks.

Larch Lake and Chiwaukum Mountains

Upper Index Creek valley

NASON CREEK
Alpine Lakes Wilderness

17 INDEX CREEK– PAINTER CREEK LOOP

Loop trip 24¼ miles
Allow 3–4 days
High point 6700 feet
Elevation gain 4000 feet
Hikable August through mid-
September

Maps: Green Trails No. 177
Chiwaukum Mountains and No.
178 Leavenworth
Current information: Ask at
Leavenworth Ranger Station
about trail Nos. 1570, 1571, 1572,
and 1575

Peaceful valley forests, flowery alpine meadows, waterfalls and high ridges, tremendous views, and considerable solitude—who could ask for anything more? Don't complain about the absence of bridges at several crucial stream crossings—they keep out the hikers who aren't serious.

Drive to the Chiwaukum Creek trailhead, elevation 1800 feet (see Hike 15 for directions).

Hike South Fork Chiwaukum Creek trail No. 1571 to a junction at 7 miles, 3700 feet, with Painter Creek trail, the return leg of the loop (Hike 18). Continue past camps at Timothy Meadows to the takeoff of Index Creek trail No. 1572 at 8½ miles, 4100 feet (Hike 18).

Index Creek trail receives little use and less maintenance; from a narrow slot thigh-high in greenery, it plunges into head-high brush. Push through to South Fork Chiwaukum Creek and wade, ford, splash, or (in late summer) leap across.

The way climbs steadily 1 mile to a crossing of Index Creek, enters forest and trail-bog, and at about 2 miles from the Chiwaukum trail levels out in a broad beaver meadow, the dams abandoned but the ponds remaining. In the next ¾ mile, the way passes several camps, leaves meadows, and recrosses the creek. At 2¾ miles from South Fork Chiwaukum Creek (11 miles from the road-end) is the intersection with Icicle Ridge trail No. 1570, 4800 feet (Hike 19).

Turn left and climb from dense pine forest to subalpine fir forest to sparse larch forest to fields of flowers, with views east to Cape Horn and Ladies Pass. Gaining 1900 feet in 1½ miles, reach the crest of a sharp ridge at 6700 feet, and then drop abruptly to little Carter Lake, 6160 feet. The trail disappears in meadows; cross a small stream and proceed straight ahead, keeping the lake to the left, passing boggy camps strongly favored by mosquitoes and no-see-ums. The trail now reappears. Cross another small creek to the Painter Creek trail intersection, 2 miles from Index Creek (13½ miles from the road-end), elevation 6200 feet.

Recross the small creek and head down the trough of Painter Creek (Hike 18). At 5½ miles from Carter Lake, where The Badlands trail crosses Painter Creek, the Painter Creek trail plunges over the brink of the hanging trough and plummets down. The valley narrows and the path, cleverly laced between cliffs in a series of traverses, drops 2½ miles to South Fork Chiwaukum Creek, which must be forded to close the loop at 8 miles from Carter Lake, a total of 20 miles from the start. The Chiwaukum River is followed the final 5½ miles back to the starting point.

For a longer loop, skip Index Creek, continue on the South Fork Chiwaukum trail to Ladies Pass, and there turn left on Icicle Ridge trail to Painter Creek, a journey of 5 to 6 days with several thousand feet more elevation gain but only some 6 more miles.

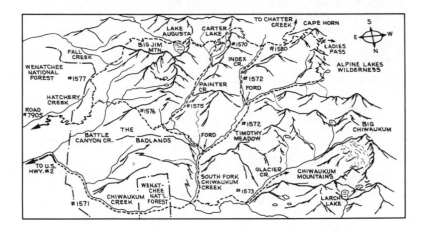

18 LAKE AUGUSTA

Round trip to Lake Augusta 18 miles
Allow 2–3 days
High point 6854 feet
Elevation gain 4000 feet in, 350 feet out
Hikable mid-July through September
Loop trip through The Badlands 23 miles
Allow 3–4 days

High point 7300 feet
Elevation gain 7000 feet
Hikable August through mid-September
Map: Green Trails No. 177 Chiwaukum Mountains
Current information: Ask at Leavenworth Ranger Station about trail Nos. 1570, 1576, and 1577

A spur ridge juts 4 miles north from Icicle Ridge, crags and tundra on its crest, lakes filling meadow cirques scooped from its flanks, forests in deep-green valleys below. Lake Augusta is the star of the waters, the meadow basin so popular that parts of the trail have been beaten to dust by hooves and boots, other parts to mud. Big Jim Mountain, 7763 feet, is the star of the skies, urgently calling lovers of those tiny alpine flowers that eke out existence among stones.

Drive US 2 to the Wenatchee River bridge opposite Tumwater Campground and turn west on Hatchery Creek road No. 7905, passing summer homes. At 1.2 and 2.2 miles stay right at unmarked forks. At 3 miles is a stub going off right to a parking area, elevation 2800 feet.

Hatchery Creek trail No. 1577 sets out on a stiff climb through brush of an old clearcut, switchbacks up open forest, and at 2¼ miles crosses a dribble of a creek, one of the few watering holes in these parts; on a knoll a few steps beyond is a three-sleeping-bag camp, 4600 feet, giving grand views over the Wenatchee River valley. At 3 miles, 5300 feet, the trail splits. The Badlands trail No. 1576, return leg of the loop, goes right.

The Hatchery Creek trail continues leftward, the angle relenting to be-

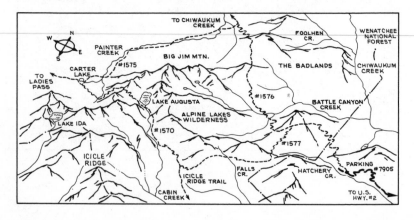

Lake Augusta

gin a rollercoaster through parkland and gardens. At 5½ miles, 6300 feet, at the headwaters of Falls Creek, is a memorable camp on a rocky promontory pinkened by lewisia, besides a gaudiness of spring-fed blossoms. On the ridge crest at 6½ miles, 6700 feet, is a junction with Icicle Ridge trail No. 1570 (Hike 19). Turn right, drop to 6350 feet, pass above horse-stomped camps in the meadows of Cabin Creek, and finish the climb to Lake Augusta, 9 miles, 6854 feet. Horses and fires are not permitted. Any true friend of the fragile land will camp well away from the lake, where meadow restoration is in progress.

A hiker must not come this far without following the trail up to the 7300-foot tundra saddle in Big Jim Mountain for long views to Mt. Rainier and close views of the Chiwaukum Mountains.

To loop on out via The Badlands, descend from the saddle to the vanishment of tread in meadows. Get out the map to determine which way the trail goes, and upon reentering forest watch for blazes; distrust bootprints, most of which are of lost hikers being led astray by animals. At 1½ miles from Lake Augusta are boggy little Carter Lake, 6160 feet, several boggy camps, and the junction with Painter Creek trail No. 1575 (Hike 17). Turn right down the broad trough of Painter Creek, fording the stream six times, passing many pleasant camps. The fields of grass are knee-high, Big Jim hulks high above, and an awesomely long willow swamp occupies a filled-in lake basin excavated by a very ancient glacier.

From the final ford at 5200 feet, 7 miles from Lake Augusta and 16 miles from the start of the hike, turn uphill on The Badlands trail, climbing steeply to a grassy ridge crest, 6200 feet, wondering about the whereabouts of whatever it is that is supposed to be bad about The Badlands. Wind on over the ridge and down to Battle Canyon Creek, 18 miles, and a spookily lonesome and thoroughly enchanting campsite. Climb 1 mile back to Hatchery Creek trail to close the loop.

19   ICICLE RIDGE

**Round trip to Lake Augusta
36 miles
Allow 3–4 days
High point 7029 feet
Elevation gain 8000 feet in, 2500
feet out
Hikable (in part) May through mid-
October**

**Maps: Green Trails No. 177
Chiwaukum Mountains and No.
178 Leavenworth
Current information: Ask at
Leavenworth Ranger Station
about trail No. 1570**

No hiker of spirit cannot but aspire to set out from the edge of Leavenworth, climb to the crest of Icicle Ridge, and walk the skyline to Big Jim Mountain and Lake Augusta and onward to Ladies Pass, Snowgrass Mountain, and Frosty Pass. Many (*very* many) hikers do indeed glory in the meadows and lakes of the latter part of Icicle Ridge trail. However, the earlier stretch, though just as scenic and paradoxically much wilder, is bone dry after the end of snowmelt and thus rarely hiked. All the better for solitude, and not too thirsty if done when patches of snow linger.

The disaster threatening this splendid ridge is—as everywhere hereabouts—the Northern Pacific Land Grant. Though Longview Fibre never built any railroads, it has acquired several grant sections on the ridge and plans to build a logging road that would ruin the trail and open the fragile crest to motorized havoc. If not permitted a direct switchbacking access, the company intends to contour around from farther up Icicle Creek, sparing the trail yet still opening lonesome highlands to fun machines. Any innocent who supposes the Alpine Lakes Wilderness is "complete" had better think again.

From US 2 on the west outskirts of Leavenworth, drive south 1.4 miles on Icicle Creek road, go right on a bit of old highway, and in 0.1 mile find Icicle Ridge trail No. 1570, elevation 1200 feet.

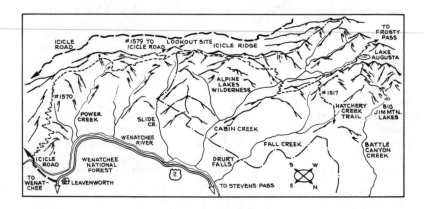

The start truly tests hikers, climbing 1600 feet in 2 miles to the ridge crest and continuing to climb as the crest aims for the sky. At 6 miles, 5200 feet, the angle eases somewhat, though by no means becoming flat. Views begin and at 8 miles meadows. At 9 miles the way passes the Fourth of July Creek trail (Hike 24) and the site of Icicle Ridge Lookout, 7029 feet, highest point of the route. Really thirsty hikers may be interested to learn that the lookout used to fetch water from a small spring about 1400 vertical feet down the trail from his cabin.

Going down more than up, the ridge trail follows the crest another 2½ miles before dropping to Cabin Creek at 13 miles, 5000 feet, and the first certain all-summer water. The way ascends from the valley to a meadowy ridge paralleling Icicle Ridge (whose crest is not regained until Ladies Pass), at 16½ miles, 6700 feet, passes Hatchery Creek trail (Hike 17), and at 18 miles attains Lake Augusta, 6854 feet.

The Icicle Ridge trail proceeds over two high passes (Hikes 17 and 18), rounds a shoulder of Cape Horn to Ladies Pass, and ends at Frosty Pass (Hike 33), 24 miles from that spirited beginning.

Mount Stuart from Icicle Ridge

Glacier-polished rock and Lake Viviane

20 ENCHANTMENT LAKES

Round trip to Snow Lakes 13½ miles
Allow 2 days
High point 5415 feet
Elevation gain 3800 feet
Hikable July through October
Round trip to Lower Enchantment Lakes 20 miles
Allow 3–4 days
High point 7000 feet

Elevation gain 5400 feet
Hikable late July through mid-October
Map: Green Trails No. 209S The Enchantments
Current information: Ask at Leavenworth Ranger Station about trail No. 1553
Forest Service permit required

A legendary group of lakes in rock basins over 7000 feet high amid the Cashmere Crags of the Stuart Range; one of the most famous places in the Cascade Mountains. Large lakes, small ponds, gigantic slabs of ice-polished granite, flower gardens, heather meadows, trees gnarled and twisted by the elements, waterfalls, snowfields, and glaciers. Visit in summer for flowers, in late September to see the autumn gold of larch. This is not a trip for beginners. The way is long, steep, and grueling. A strong hiker needs at least 12 hours to reach the high lakes. The average hiker takes 2 days. The rest never make it.

It also is not a trip for hermits. Thanks to a Forest Service limit on entry permits, the scene no longer is disgustingly mobbed but always is busy. If you decide to come anyhow, be prepared to obey as strict a moral code as any in American wilderness. The fragility of the vegetation requires it. So does the reduced but still considerable population density. Motorcycles were the first superconsumers to be prohibited. Then came horses. And then, *dogs*—do not expect law-abiding hikers to accept your excuse that "Gee, I never go no place without good ol' Slasher." Bring a stove—wood fires are banned. Camp on bare ground at established sites. Look for those less used, away from the main trail. Use toilets where provided. Boil your water. Walk on rock or snow rather than plants. Limit party size to six. If you can't live with all that, do without the hike.

From US 2 on the west outskirts of Leavenworth, drive south 4 miles on Icicle Creek road and turn left into the Snow Lakes trail parking area, elevation 1400 feet.

Snow Lakes trail No. 1553 crosses the river and immediately starts up—and up. The way switchbacks in forest, with views in the early part to the granite cliffs of Snow Creek Wall. Small camps at approximately 2 miles, 2800 feet, offer a break in the journey for parties wishing to make the approach in easy stages. At 5½ miles is Nada Lake, 5000 feet, and good camps. At 6¾ miles the trail passes between the two Snow Lakes at 5415 feet. For camping here, find sites to the left at the lower lake and all the way around the left side of the upper lake to where the trail finally starts up. To the north rises 8292-foot Temple and to the south 8364-foot Mt. McClellan. All beginners and most average hikers find this far enough, and these lakes magnificent enough.

Little Annapurna and Snow Creek Glacier from Gnome Tarn

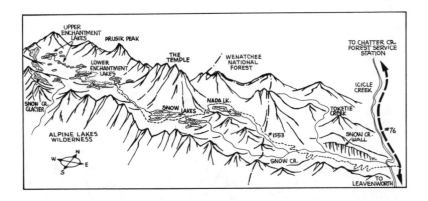

To continue to the Enchantments, cross the low dam between the two lakes. Pause to note this rather weird interference with nature: like a bathtub, water is drained through a hole in the bottom of the upper lake (which thus has a fluctuating shoreline) and is used to guarantee a pure intake for the Leavenworth Fish Hatchery; probably few people imagined, when the project was perpetrated back in the 1930s, that Snow Lakes would become as popular as they are.

Follow the trail winding along the left shore. At the south end cross the inlet stream and proceed up Snow Creek, climbing into granite country. At 10 miles reach Lake Viviane, 6800 feet.

The area was discovered by A. H. Sylvester, a topographer for the U.S. Geological Survey for some 13 years and then, from 1908 to 1931, supervisor of Wenatchee National Forest. In his years of exploring, he placed thousands of names on maps of the West. "Enchantment" expressed his reaction—and that of all who have followed. The one name covered everything until climbers arrived in the late 1940s and began assigning names to "The Crags." Then came Bill and Peg Stark, who over many years drew on various mythologies to name the lakes and other features. A lake and its swordlike rock peninsula became Lake Viviane and Excalibur Rock. Other lakes and tarns they called Rune, Talisman, Valkyrie, Leprechaun, Naiad, Lorelei, Dryad, Pixie, Gnome, Brisingamen, Brynhild, Reginleif, Sprite, and Titania. And there is Troll Sink (a pond), Valhalla Cirque, Tanglewood, and many more.

Lower Enchantment Basin, at and around 7000 feet, is friendliest. Upper Enchantment Basin, at and around 7500 feet, is a splendidly raw desolation, the earth not yet fully created. Some of its lakes are clear and some are jade-colored by rock milk and some are frozen solid all summer. When Sylvester was here—not all that long ago—nearly the whole basin was occupied by the Snow Creek Glacier.

21 LAKE CAROLINE

Round trip 11 miles
Hiking time 8 hours
High point 6190 feet
Elevation gain 2870 feet
Hikable mid-July through
October
One day or backpack

Map: Green Trails No. 209S The
Enchantments
Current information: Ask at
Leavenworth Ranger Station
about trail Nos. 1552
and 1554

Another famous attraction of the Alpine Lakes Wilderness, a high, tree-ringed lake, meadows, and a wealth of cliffs. A special treat is the great north face of 9415-foot Mt. Stuart, seen from close enough to make out crevasses in the hanging glaciers.

The trail to Lake Caroline crosses the checkerboard ownership inherited from the railroad land grant. The present owners are "reducing their inventory" before new legislation curtails frontier-style savagery, and in the first 1½ miles the trail is disrupted in several places.

From US 2 on the west outskirts of Leavenworth, drive 8.5 miles south on Icicle Creek road and turn left across a bridge on road No. 7601 up Eightmile Creek, climbing steeply 3 more miles to the trailhead, elevation 3320 feet.

Eightmile Lake trail No. 1552, on the uphill side of the road, is clearly signed. The trail ascends moderately, following Eightmile Creek, with about ½ mile of road-walking. At 2½ miles the way reaches Little Eightmile Lake, 4400 feet, and a junction. The left fork goes another ½ mile up the valley to 4641-foot Eightmile Lake and good camps. The lake is ringed by woods but awesome rock walls rise far above the trees.

The right fork of trail No. 1554 climbs an endless series of switchbacks (hot and thirsty on sunny days) from the valley, first in timber, then emerging to meadows. The labor is rewarded by steadily improving views

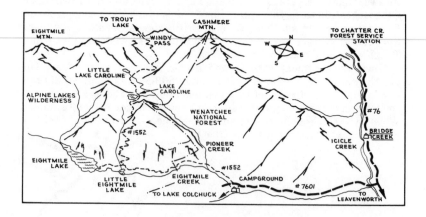

Lake Caroline and Cashmere Mountain

to the jagged spires of the Stuart Range and finally the tall thrust of Mt. Stuart itself. At 5½ miles is the alpine basin of Lake Caroline, 6190 feet. The most attractive campsites are ½ mile farther and 200 feet higher at Little Lake Caroline, surrounded by meadows.

The best is yet to come. The 2-mile hike to 7200-foot Windy Pass, on good trail amid flowers and larches, is an absolute must. For broader views, walk the ridge toward 8501-foot Cashmere Mountain—but don't try for the summit; the last pitches are strictly for climbers.

To preserve vegetation, campers are asked to use only established campsites.

22 LAKE STUART– COLCHUCK LAKE

Round trip to Colchuck Lake 9 miles
Hiking time 8 hours
High point 5570 feet
Elevation gain 2000 feet
Hikable mid-July through October
One day or backpack
Round trip to Lake Stuart 9 miles
Hiking time 7 hours

High point 5064 feet
Elevation gain 1500 feet
Hikable mid-July through October
One day or backpack
Map: Green Trails No. 209S The Enchantments
Current information: Ask at Leavenworth Ranger Station about trail Nos. 1599 and 1599A
Forest Service permit required

Two large lakes amid subalpine forests and granite cliffs of the Stuart Range. Hike to emerald waters of Colchuck Lake and contemplate towering crags above, decorated with two small glaciers. Or, to cure itchy feet, visit nearby Lake Stuart. Or, if it's peace and quiet you want, don't come here at all because this is the most heavily used trail and lake system in the vicinity—even more so than the Enchantments!

From Icicle Creek road drive 4 miles on road No. 7601 (Hike 21) to the trailhead, elevation 3400 feet. Find Lake Stuart–Colchuck Lake trail No. 1599 at a sharp turn of the road on the creek side.

The trail parallels Mountaineer Creek on a constant upward grade for 1 mile, and then switchbacks up the steepening valley to a junction at 2½ miles, 4500 feet.

The left trail (a rough path) crosses Mountaineer Creek and ascends with many switchbacks, in open forest among numerous granite knolls,

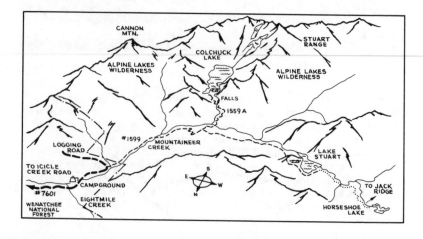

Lake Stuart and Mount Stuart

along the cascading waters of East Fork Mountaineer Creek. During the final ¼ mile, the way passes a waterfall, leaves the creek, and comes to a tiny, almost landlocked lagoon of Colchuck Lake, 5570 feet, 4½ miles. Incredibly, this lovely blue-green lake, like others in the area, is drained for use by the Icicle Irrigation District. Camping all the way around the right side of the lake. Note: Dogs are not allowed on this trail.

The right trail (notorious as probably the doggiest in the Cascades) proceeds gently up the main fork of Mountaineer Creek to the wooded shores, clear blue water, and tall cliffs of Lake Stuart, 5064 feet, 4½ miles. Campsites near the point where the trail first reaches the lake. Follow the trail ¼ mile beyond the lake to a marshy meadow under the towering cliffs of Mt. Stuart. Beyond lies *wild* wilderness, brushy and craggy, mean and dangerous; Horseshoe Lake and Jack Ridge are strictly for the superdoughty.

To preserve the vegetation, campers are asked to use established sites at either lake. No fires; carry a stove.

23 AASGARD PASS

Round trip to lower Enchantment Lakes 15 miles
Allow 3–4 days
High point 7750 feet
Elevation gain 4410 feet in, 670 feet out
Scrambleable August through mid-September

Map: Green Trails No. 209S The Enchantments
Current information: Ask at Leavenworth Ranger Station about trail No. 1599
Forest Service permit required

Three things often are said to be radically wrong with the Snow Lakes route to the Enchantments (Hike 20): too many miles and too much elevation and, when you get there, too many people. Myth has it that the Colchuck Lake approach, pioneered by climbers aiming at peaks of the Dragontail group, is an easy shortcut and has solitude to boot. Don't believe it. Four things are terribly wrong with the entry via Aasgard Pass: It's not easy; actually it's a climbers' route, usually requiring an ice ax, sometimes rope and crampons, and in early summer the ability to recognize avalanche instability. It's dangerous, not only from falling off cliffs or slippery boulders or snowfields or from being fallen upon by snow or rock, but also from summer storms that at these elevations can be distinctly hypothermic and from summer snowfalls that can make the already difficult descent of boulder fields a very long nightmare. It's not esthetic—instead of ascending ritually and respectfully from the picturesque lower

New moraine left by retreating glacier in Upper Enchantment Lakes

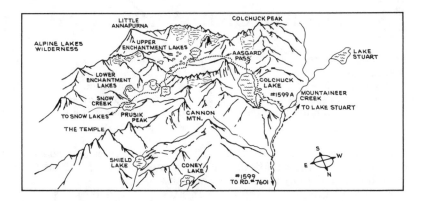

basin to the austere upper basin and at last to the cold snows and stern stones of Aasgard, one does it all backward, like starting with the ice cream and working through the meatballs and potatoes to the soup. Finally, when you get to the Enchantments the people are already there, never fear.

Why, then, is the route in this book? As a warning against myths. To save the innocent from being suckered in by "the easy way to the Enchantments." Also to quash the faddy notion that this is the classy and sassy way, the route of the big kids. For anyone it's a tasteless route. For hikers lacking climbing equipment and training, it's a route silly to the point of suicidal.

If determined to go this dangerous way, drive to the Lake Stuart–Colchuck Lake trailhead, elevation 3400 feet, and hike 4½ miles to Colchuck Lake, 5570 feet (Hike 22).

Round the shore to the right, to a camping area where formal trail ends and boulder-hopping begins. Ascend under the Colchuck Glacier on the side of Colchuck Peak, over talus from Colchuck Col, and beneath Dragontail Peak to slopes below Aasgard Pass.

The ascent is the next thing to vertical, gaining 2200 feet in ¾ mile on small rocks that slide under the boot and large rocks that in rain or snow the boot skids on. Watch for cairns placed by the Forest Service, a practice generally unacceptable in the wilderness but necessary here to keep neophytes from straying into the cliffs. About two-thirds of the way, cross to the right under a knot of trees and rocks and follow cairns over a small stream and a snowfield to the pass, 7800 feet.

You and your heavy pack are now at a nobly arctic and splendidly scenic lunch stop and climactic turnaround point for hikers exploring (with rucksack loads only) upward from camps in the comfort of the lower basin. However, to enjoy a cozy night you must traverse the upper basin, a joy to the eye but pleasantly campable only in the most benign conditions, and descend past the meatballs to the potatoes and, in grim weather, even to the soup. But be of good cheer: you don't have to climb back to Aasgard in that raging storm. As more than one "shortcut" party has learned, via Snow Creek trail and road it's only 18 miles back to your car.

24 FOURTH OF JULY CREEK

Round trip 13 miles
Hiking time 8 hours
High point 7000 feet
Elevation gain 4800 feet
Hikable May (in part) through
  October

One day or backpack
Map: Green Trails No. 177
  Chiwaukum Mountains
Current information: Ask at
  Leavenworth Ranger Station
  about trail No. 1579

In all the Icicle country, the Fourth of July trail is the best day hike to high views of Mt. Stuart, Mt. Cashmere, the meadowy-craggy length of Icicle Ridge, and bulky ramparts of the Chiwaukum Mountains. If the 4600 feet all the way to the old lookout site exceed the available musclepower, panoramas are proportionately rewarding three-quarters or even halfway up, and this much of the trail, on a southerly exposure as it is, can be done before June, when the floral display of this rainshadow side of the Cascades is in its best weeks of the year.

From US 2 on the west outskirts of Leavenworth, drive south on the Icicle Creek road. At 8.5 miles pass Eightmile Creek junction and at 9.4 miles find a small paved parking area and Fourth of July trail No. 1579, elevation 2200 feet.

The trailhead sign gives the distance as 5 miles; it feels like 7 or 8; we've compromised on 6. The trail wastes little time getting down (or up) to business, in ¼ mile crossing the creek (the last certain water) and addressing a series of short switchbacks that will numb your mind if you try to count them. Focus instead on the flowers and on the views that begin as window glimpses and grow to wide screen, especially to 8501-foot Cashmere Mountain directly across the Icicle valley.

A mile below the ridge crest, the way quits the zigzag and begins a traversing ascent eastward. At about 5400 feet is a spring where the fire lookout used to come for water, though maybe not by summer's end. Due to the scarcity of water on this sunny south slope, rattlesnakes gather from miles around to have a sip and cool off in the grass and mud, so don't be too greedy.

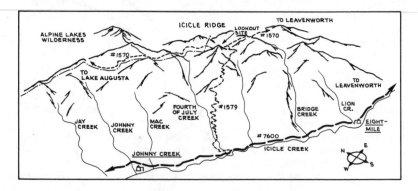

Mount Stuart Range from Fourth of July trail

At 6800 feet, about 6 miles, the path attains the crest and joins Icicle Ridge trail No. 1570 (Hike 19). Ascend a final ¼ mile to the lookout site, 7029 feet. The cabin was perched atop a rock thumb and was reached by ladder. Cabin and ladder are gone and the thumb is difficult. Never mind—the view from the bottom is as good as from the top.

25 JACK CREEK–TROUT LAKE

Loop trip 13 miles
Hiking time 7 hours
High point 5800 feet
Elevation gain 3000 feet in, 1000
feet out
Hikable mid-July through mid-
October

One day or backpack
Map: Green Trails No. 177
    Chiwaukum Mountains
Current information: Ask at
    Leavenworth Ranger Station
    about trail Nos. 1557 and 1558

Miles of virgin forest lead to a lake tucked in narrow Trout Creek valley between the walls of Eightmile Mountain and Jack Ridge. The lake is in the Alpine Lake Wilderness, but a big hunk of the valley, land that was part of the Northern Pacific Railroad land grant, is at the mercy of private timber companies engaged in exporting America's natural beauty overseas. The Trout Creek trail remains open to travel but the Forest Service no longer maintains it. The recommended route, longer with a lot of elevation gain, is an excellent forest walk.

Drive the Icicle Creek road (Hike 24) some 17 miles to Rock Island Campground, cross the cement bridge, and in 0.1 mile turn left on road No. (6800)615. Go 0.2 mile more and find the Jack Creek trailhead parking area on the right side of the road, elevation 2800 feet.

Jack Creek trail No. 1558 traverses a clearcut, in ¼ mile crosses Jack Creek on a steel bridge, and then leaves the creek and climbs through forest to join the original trail, whose beginning stretch from Chatter Creek is now abandoned. At approximately 2½ miles is a junction. The straight-ahead trail follows Jack Creek to Meadow Creek and Van Epps trails. Go left on trail No. 1557, climbing endless switchbacks to a 5790-foot high point on Jack Ridge at 5 miles, then going down, down, down more switchbacks, losing 1000 feet, to the Trout Creek valley and the outlet of Trout Lake, 4800 feet, at about 6½ miles.

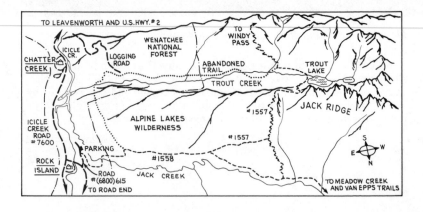

If the abandoned trail has not been completely obliterated (check with ranger), a loop can be made up Trout Creek to the lake, over Jack Ridge, and down Jack Creek.

Jack Creek bridge

Lake Edna

ICICLE CREEK
Alpine Lakes Wilderness

26 CHATTER CREEK–LAKE EDNA

Round trip to Chatter Creek Basin 5 miles
Hiking time 3 hours
High point 5300 feet
Elevation gain 2500 feet
Hikable July through mid-September
One day or backpack
Round trip to Lake Edna 11½ miles
Hiking time 8 hours

High point 6750 feet
Elevation gain 3750 feet
Hikable mid-July through mid-September
One day or backpack
Map: Green Trails No. 177 Chiwaukum Mountains
Current information: Ask at Leavenworth Ranger Station about trail No. 1580

The Chatter Creek trail is a quick, though by no means easy, way to the much-beloved alpine realm of "Mormon Ladies Lakes," by legend (but not historical fact) named for the many wives of Brigham Young. However, the creek's headwaters cirque beneath rugged walls of Grindstone Mountain is delight enough for a day, and a spectacular highland traverse leads to Lake Edna, lonesomest and perhaps prettiest of the ladies.

Drive the Icicle Creek road (Hike 24) 15.8 miles, to 0.3 mile past Chatter Creek Campground, and then go off right 0.1 mile on the sideroad to Chatter Creek trail No. 1580, elevation 2800 feet.

The trail starts on an old road through a brushy clearcut, in 100 yards splitting; go right. In $1/4$ mile the road quits and, after passing a hunters' camp at the end of the logging, the trail goes to work, climbing open forest along Chatter Creek 1400 feet in the next $1^1/4$ miles, then crossing the creek and rounding a corner to enter the upper, hanging valley. In a final $1/2$ mile, the steepness of the angle relents and the path levels to enter the open basin. Near timberline at $2^1/2$ miles, 5300 feet, a little exploration leads to two small campsites, scenic spots for day-hikers to eat their pea-nut-butter-and-jelly sandwiches while gazing over the Icicle valley to Trout Creek and Eightmile Mountain and over Jack Ridge to Blackjack Ridge and Bootjack Mountain.

The trail switchbacks steeply across a 6800-foot rubble shoulder of Grindstone Mountain at $3^1/2$ miles and descends to glorious headwater meadows of Index Creek and several campsites, 6400 feet. Follow rock cairns and faint trail left over a boulder field, contouring to a second, larger basin below Cape Horn, where the trail disappears. Descend to a large cairn at the base of the meadow, cross a small stream, and then head uphill through a band of trees to an open rib. Hike up the rib to the edge of an upper basin, then go to the right, crossing another small stream, and scramble straight uphill and follow a now-visible bootpath the final last push to reach Icicle Ridge trail No. 1570 (Hike 19) at $5^1/2$ miles.

Go left in meadows, over buttresses of ice-polished-and-gouged rock, to snowy-stony, austerely beautiful Lake Edna, $5^3/4$ miles, 6735 feet. The camps are small and naked to the storm winds that swirl around the summit of Cape Horn, close above, but in a calm summer night, wonderful for quiet dreams.

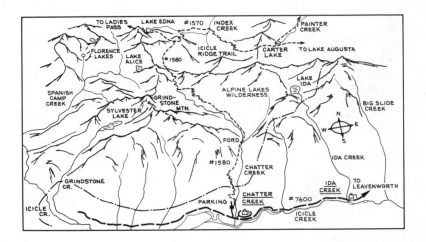

27 BLACKJACK RIDGE

Round trip to open meadows 6
  miles
Hiking time 5 hours
High point 6100 feet
Elevation gain 3250 feet
Hikable mid-July through mid-
  September
One day or backpack

Map: Green Trails No. 177
  Chiwaukum Mountains (full trail
  not shown)
Current information: Ask at
  Leavenworth Ranger Station
  about trail No. 1565

Views are superb over the Icicle valley to Icicle Ridge and Grindstone
Mountain, to the isolated mass of Cashmere Mountain and the impressive
northwest face of Mt. Stuart, and to the lonesome length of Sixtysix Hundred Ridge. There is solitude, too, for reasons: The trail is extremely steep
and fails to hold hard-won elevation but goes upsy-downsy along the
ridge, spots level enough for a sleeping bag are few, and water is scarcer
yet. If the trail is combined in a loop with the Snowall–Cradle Lake trip
(Hike 31), it is most wisely chosen as the exit rather than the entry. This
is an option reserved for expert routefinders only; the trail is so little used
it virtually disappears in Pablo Creek Basin.

Drive Icicle Creek road (Hike 24) 19.2 miles to just before the crossing
of Black Pine Creek, 300 feet before a horse-loading ramp, and on the uphill side of the road find trail No. 1565, elevation 2850 feet. (If you reach
the end of the Icicle Creek road, you've gone ¼ mile too far.)

The trail starts in an area of selective logging (all the big, beautiful
trees selected, otherwise known as "high-grading") but in ¼ mile enters
the Alpine Lakes Wilderness and commences switchbacks that seem
steeper at each turn and appear unlikely ever to end this side of the
moon. However, in 2¾ miles the ascent gentles in open meadows atop
Blackjack Ridge. The trail skims through fragile flowers to a high point of

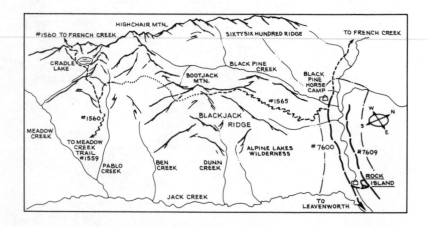

Icicle Ridge from Bootjack Mountain

6100 feet, 3 miles, on the shoulder of 6789-foot Bootjack Mountain. Here is the first view of the great wall of Mt. Stuart and a proper place for day-hikers to suck their dusty canteens before heading home.

Day-hikers should be satisfied with looking into the green basin below the 6100-foot shoulder of Bootjack Mountain. However, if after climbing 3300 feet there is still energy left, follow the ridge upward on a faint path through forest and meadows with expanding views. The ridge is blocked twice by rocky outcrops. Go right of the first pyramid-shaped rock and left of the second jumbled mess to the rocky summit of 6789-foot Bootjack Mountain. The final 70 feet takes a bit of scramble not recommended for hikers without mountaineering experience.

28 ICICLE CREEK

Round trip to Josephine Lake	**Maps: Green Trails No. 176 Stevens**
22½ miles	**Pass and No. 177 Chiwaukum**
Allow 2–3 days	**Mountains**
High point 4681 feet	**Current information: Ask at**
Elevation gain 1780 feet	**Leavenworth Ranger Station**
Hikable July through mid-	**about trail No. 1551**
October	

The Icicle Creek trail is the main arterial of the northeast sector of the Alpine Lakes Wilderness. It leads to almost everywhere, hooks up tributary trails for all manner of loops, in itself is a splendid route through deep forest to deep blue waters of Josephine Lake and gardens of the Cascade Crest, and has frequent pleasant camps beside the stream that make the lower stretches extremely popular with families introducing children to backpacking. In the upper stretches the maintenance is spotty and at places hikers must burrow through over-the-head brush.

Drive the Icicle Creek road (Hike 24) 17.5 miles to a split at Rock Island Campground. Go left 1.9 miles on road No. 7600 to the end and Icicle Creek trailhead No. 1551, elevation 2880 feet.

The trail rolls through quiet forest 1¼ miles to super-popular French Creek Camp, crosses French Creek to more campsites, and meets a junction with French Creek trail (Hike 29). Continue along the Icicle to the next junction, 1½ miles, with the French Ridge trail (Hike 30). A scant ½ mile beyond, pass the Frosty Creek–Wildhorse trail (Hike 33). Near 4 miles is the unsigned start of the long-abandoned Doughgod Creek trail; though shown on maps its lower stretch has vanished in brush and in any event is inaccessible across unbridged Icicle Creek.

At 4½ miles pass a large camp and cross Icicle Creek on a bridge to more camps, 3080 feet, ascend briefly, cross two very brushy avalanche paths, and at a third campsite come to the Leland Creek junction, 6 miles, 3240 feet (camps on both sides of Icicle Creek but no trace of vanished Bark Cabin), and the takeoff for Hikes 34 and 35.

At 7½ miles, 3400 feet, something dramatic happens. To here the val-

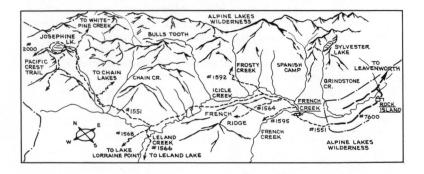

ley has been wide and the floor virtually flat, the trail the next thing to level, and the creek generally quiet, with many succulent swimming pools. But here, where in ancient times lesser glaciers gathered into one mighty glacier, performing the usual job of grinding the valley down at the heel, the trail must climb, and it does, switchbacking a steep step upward into a narrower hanging valley, at 8½ miles, 3800 feet, passing Chain Lakes trail (Hike 10).

The upper valley attained, the trail flattens a bit, passing another camp in the woods, recrossing Icicle Creek at 9 miles, and at 10½ miles reaching the Whitepine trail, 4400 feet. At last the way emerges into subalpine meadows on a final climb to the cirque of Josephine Lake, 11¼ miles, 4681 feet, and much-used camps.

A final ¾-mile ascent of heather meadows reaches the end of the Icicle Creek trail at the Pacific Crest Trail, 5000 feet. Should a one-way hike be the party's intent, an easy 4 miles lead to Stevens Pass (Hike 9).

Josephine Lake

29 FRENCH CREEK

**Round trip to Meadow Creek
Pass 24 miles
Allow 2–3 days
High point 5320 feet
Elevation gain 2400 feet plus
many ups and downs
Hikable July through mid-
October**

**Maps: Green Trails No. 176 Stevens
Pass and No. 177 Chiwaukum
Mountains
Current information: Ask at
Leavenworth Ranger Station
about trail No. 1595**

When the famous valleys grow crowded, obscure valleys grow the more appealing. French Creek has green forests and white water and cozy camps to keep hikers smiling quietly in their solitude. However, the trail isn't totally lonesome because it does have a degree of fame as an access to alpine lakes and meadows.

Drive Icicle Creek road (Hike 24) to the end, elevation 2880 feet.

Hike the Icicle Creek trail 1¼ miles to French Creek trail No. 1595, 2900 feet (Hike 28). Also signed "Backdoor Trail," the way follows the north bank of the creek. At about 3 miles (from the Icicle Creek road) admire the monstrous swath of an avalanche that swept down the opposite ridge, across the valley bottom, and 200 feet up this side of the valley to the trail. *There* was a spectacle that would have made the day for a party of cross-country skiers or snowshoers.

At 3¾ miles pass a nice (and popular) campsite. At 5 miles is the south end of French Ridge and the takeoff of Backdoor trail No. 1564A, presumably so named at this end to distinguish it from the north end of the same trail, at that end called "French Ridge Trail" (Hike 30). At 6 miles are the confluence of French and Snowall Creeks, another good camp, and the

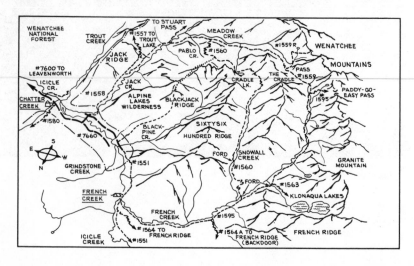

French Creek

start of Cradle Lake trail No. 1560 (Hike 31).

At 7¼ miles are a camp and a difficult crossing of Klonaqua Creek. Small logs upstream may perhaps be scooted; otherwise the feet must be got wet, and the knees, and possibly the hips. That done, pass the start of Klonaqua Lakes trail No. 1563 (Hike 32), 3700 feet. Since that's the destination of nearly everyone who travels the French Creek trail, the solitude now deepens, down in shadowy forest where rarely is the contemplation of greenery disturbed by glimpses of high snowfields and peaks or sky.

From here on, the path is populated by more (almost) horses than people and is consequently mudholed and root-tangled. At 11 miles the trail turns uphill to Paddy-Go-Easy Pass (Hikes 73 and 74), crossing the ridge to the Cle Elum River valley. Stay on the French Creek trail, which now becomes No. 1559. At 12 miles the trail tops out on the wooded flat of Meadow Creek Pass, 5220 feet, in itself not much of a destination, but the way continues as Meadow Creek trail No. 1559, dropping past a sidetrail to Pablo Basin and Cradle Lake (a loop! a loop!) to Jack Creek and on down to the Icicle Creek road (another loop!).

French Ridge

ICICLE CREEK
Alpine Lakes Wilderness

TURQUOISE LAKE–
FRENCH RIDGE

**Round trip to Turquoise Lake 17
miles**
Allow 2 or more days
High point 3600 feet
**Elevation gain 3000 feet in, 900
feet out**
**Hikable mid-July through
September**
**Round trip to lookout site 12
miles**
Allow 2 days

High point 5800 feet
Elevation gain 3000 feet
**Hikable mid-July through
September**
**Maps: Green Trails No. 176 Stevens
Pass and No. 177 Chiwaukum
Mountains**
**Current information: Ask at
Leavenworth Ranger Station
about trail Nos. 1564, 1595, and
1564A**

When all the easy trails fill up with happy faces, mean and nasty trails
begin to beguile, especially when the ultimate rewards are a flower-rich
ridge and a sparkling lake, ¹/₃ mile long, tucked in a slender cirque so difficult to reach that crowds are too thin to deserve the name.

Drive Icicle Creek road (Hike 24) to the end, elevation 2880 feet.

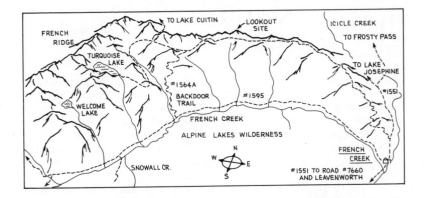

Hike 5 miles on the Icicle Creek and French Creek trails to the takeoff point of the Backdoor Trail, here signed "French Ridge Trail No. 1564," elevation 3300 feet.

Because the hike is too strenuous for most folks to do in a day and there is no dependable water from French Creek nearly to the lake, the best plan is to camp at the inviting spot beside the creek at 3¾ miles (from the road) and set out very early next morning carrying quarts of water.

The reason for suggesting a very early start becomes apparent as the steep trail gets steeper, switchbacking up a parched, south-facing slope with little shade, gaining 1500 feet in what is officially measured as 1 mile, though a person is likely to feel a zero ought to be added. Quitting the zigzags but not the climbing, the way sidehills east a long ½ mile into a small basin of subalpine trees and flowers, but no water after the snow goes. Here is an unmarked junction, 5450 feet.

The French Ridge trail proceeds straight ahead in meadows 1½ miles to a large, green meadow, former site of a lookout tower, with commanding views up and down the Icicle valley and to distant peaks. Eat your kipper snacks and drink your lemonade and admire the panoramas the lookout used to scan for smoke. From here the trail continues down to the Icicle Creek trail, a possible loop.

For Turquoise Lake go left, southwesterly, on the unsigned trail to Turquoise Lake. After a nice bit to sucker you in, the trouble begins. The way climbs 500 feet more to swing around a spur of French Ridge, then loses the 500 feet into the valley of a nameless tributary of French Creek; a delightful camp here, and water. Another 400 feet are lost getting around cliffs and rockslides of another spur ridge and 500 feet are regained to reach meager camps at the outlet of Turquoise Lake, 5465 feet, about 8½ miles from the road. One can only hope it is worth it.

SNOWALL CREEK–
CRADLE LAKE

31

Round trip 26 miles
Allow 2–3 days
High point 6300 feet
Elevation gain 3400 feet
Hikable August through
September

Maps: Green Trails No. 176 Stevens
Pass and No. 177 Chiwaukum
Mountains
Current information: Ask at
Leavenworth Ranger Station
about trail Nos. 1551, 1560, and
1595

Another thing that contributes to lonesomeness, aside from many miles and much elevation gain, is deep, swift water lacking bridge or footlog. Were it not for two such tests of courage, the flower gardens of upper Snowall Creek surely would be teeming with humanity. Should you be unlucky and find such a situation, try again earlier in summer when the snowmelt is flooding.

Drive Icicle Creek road (Hike 24) to the end, elevation 2880 feet.

Follow Icicle Creek and French Creek trails (Hike 30) to the start of Snowall Creek–Cradle Lake trail No. 1560 at 3550 feet, 6 miles from the road. Right off the bat there's a ford of French Creek, in August usually only knee-deep, and not so wide and cold, but you still might have sensations in your toes when you reach the far bank. Switchbacks gain 1000 feet in 2 miles to a second ford, deeper and swifter, of Snowall Creek; a stout pole is a help; short people should be tied to a rope and fitted with scuba gear.

The angle of ascent lies back as the way crosses numerous flower-rich meadows, some dry and some wet, combining for a maximum display of species. Views open to walls of 7467-foot The Cradle and snows on ridges at the valley head. At 2½ miles pass a well-used camp and at 4¾ miles enter a meadow ½ mile long, dominated in August by myriad blossoms of Merten's bluebells (many are pinkbells).

The trip now seems to have come to an abrupt end, the amphitheater of cliffs curving in a horseshoe from The Cradle to Highchair Mountain,

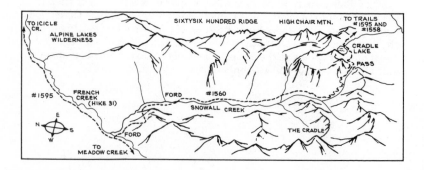

plainly a cul-de-sac. However, the trail, after semi-vanishing in bogs of a wet meadow at 5000 feet, comes out of hiding and zigs and zags and zags and zigs upward, finding an improbable cleft in the valley wall and climbing to a scenic pass, 6400 feet, in the ridge from Highchair. In ¼ mile more, drop to the flowers rimming Cradle Lake, 6200 feet, 13 miles from the Icicle road—which is to say, 13 miles the way you came. Nice camps on the ridge overlooking Meadow Creek.

Are there more people in the lake camps than you expected? That's because there's a shorter approach, via Pablo and Jack Creeks (a loop!). So maybe you should've stopped amid the bluebells of Snowall Creek, and a lovely place to stop it surely is.

Cradle Lake

32 KLONAQUA LAKES

Round trip 18 miles
Allow 2–3 days
High point 5300 feet
Elevation gain 2400 feet in, 200
feet out
Hikable mid-July through mid-
October

Map: Green Trails No. 177
Chiwaukum Mountains
Current information: Ask at
Leavenworth Ranger Station
about trail Nos. 1595 and 1563

Whatever sort of "aqua" is "klon," the two lakes of that name are among the largest splashes of blue on maps of the eastern Alpine Lakes Wilderness, and there's nothing like blue on a map to draw gangs of fishing poles, people attached. The views are as spectacular as the blueness of the aqua, up bare cliffs to snowy summits of Granite Mountain. Though, in fact, the blue of the lower lake is usually ice-white until mid-July, and of the upper until August, the trip is so popular, and sections of the path so rooty and rocky, that the trail is signed "hiker only," no horses allowed.

Drive Icicle Creek road (Hike 24) to the end, elevation 2880 feet.

Follow Icicle Creek and French Creek trails (Hike 30) to a difficult ford of Klonaqua Creek and the start of Klonaqua Lakes trail No. 1563 at 3700 feet, 7¼ miles from the road.

The trail sets right out to do its job of climbing to the fish, half the way in sight and sound of the creek, then switchbacking away into huge boulders, with several glimpses of a mighty waterfall from the cirque. At about 2 miles the path briefly levels at a camp, then ascends above a rockslide to a ridge crest at 5300 feet, and drops to lower Klonaqua Lake, 5090 feet, 9½ miles from the road.

Clumps of trees and patches of huckleberries and heather shore the lake, whose outlet was dammed in the dim past by the Icicle Irrigation

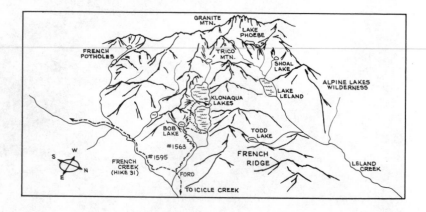

Lower Klonaqua Lake

District (for use during drought years), raising the level some 5 feet. Above the basin rise rugged summits of 7144-foot Granite Mountain.

To reach the upper lake, 5187 feet, take the fishermen's path steeply from the outlet, around the left side of the lake, a scant 1 mile to the narrow isthmus between the two.

Within conceivable exploring range of camps here are two dozen other lakes, in adjoining cirques draining to French and Leland Creeks, and beyond the ridge of Granite Mountain, draining to the Cle Elum River. Rude paths may be found to any big enough to support a trout. Some aren't, and that's a mercy.

Meadow near Lake Mary

ICICLE CREEK
Alpine Lakes Wilderness

33   LAKE MARY

**Round trip to Lake Mary
  16 miles
Allow 2–3 days
High point 6200 feet
Elevation gain 3300 feet
Hikable mid-July through
  October**

**Map: Green Trails No. 177
  Chiwaukum Mountains
Current information: Ask at
  Leavenworth Ranger Station
  about trail No. 1592**

If the Enchantments are the granite classic of the Alpine Lakes Wilderness, Snowgrass Mountain is the supreme green. This is the place for dreamlike wanderings along tundra ridges and through lake basins and around corners to magic surprises. But there is a price to pay: a gang of dreamers, hordes of dreamers, wandering everywhere—and many of them on horseback.

Drive Icicle Creek road (Hike 24) to the end, elevation 2880 feet.

Hike the Icicle Creek trail 2 miles to Frosty Creek–Wildhorse trail No. 1592, 3000 feet (Hike 28). Cross the creek and start up. (The bridge was missing in 1992; there is no safe crossings, and in absence of a replacement, try Chatter Creek trail, Hike 26.) Soon cross Frosty Creek. There's a dry hill coming, with many a dusty switchback. But the worst is over at 6 miles, 4900 feet, when the way emerges from trees into the little basin of Packrat Camp. At 6³/₄ miles a short sidepath drops a bit to woodsy Lake Margaret, 5409 feet; camping is very limited. At 7¹/₂ miles the trail tops Frosty Pass, 5800 feet, and opens out into meadow-and-parkland that stretches in every direction as far as eye can see. Where to start?

An unsigned, unmaintained trail contours northwest from the pass to an excellent camp and continues sketchily onward—ultimately to Doelle Lakes (Hike 10). The Wildhorse trail sidehills north, giving off-trail (meadow) access to Grace Lakes (Hike 12).

Eventually one is compelled by social pressures to join the parade east from Frosty Pass on Icicle Ridge trail No. 1570, in 1¹/₂ miles reaching the sidetrail dropping to Lake Mary, 6100 feet, a world-famous (nearly) place for a basecamp, and a superb spot it is—if you can find a vacancy. If not, climb the garden-wall trail ³/₄ mile to Mary Pass, 6900 feet, and drop ¹/₂ mile to Upper Florence Lake, 6500 feet, with the most scenic—and most weather-exposed—camps of all and probably all full-up anyhow.

Just 1¹/₄ flowery miles from Mary Pass is Ladies Pass, 6800 feet, above Lake Brigham and Lake Flora in headwaters of Chiwaukum Creek (Hike 15). In another mile, beyond the shoulder of 7315-foot Cape Horn, is Lake Edna, 6735 feet, a cold and rocky tarn (Hike 26). Spanish Camp Basin, below the trail to Ladies Pass, is well worth an afternoon and offers camping less crowded and much the snuggest in a storm; an old trail enters the basin from Upper Florence Lake. For high panoramas leave the trail at Mary Pass and strike up the way trail to the 7500-foot ridge of Snowgrass Mountain and views from Cashmere and Stuart to Monte Cristo and Glacier to Index and Baring. The several summits of the 4-mile-long mountain, the highest 8000 feet, require climbing experience and equipment, but easy hiking takes a person high enough to feel on top of the world.

To preserve vegetation, campers are asked to use established sites and not come here too often.

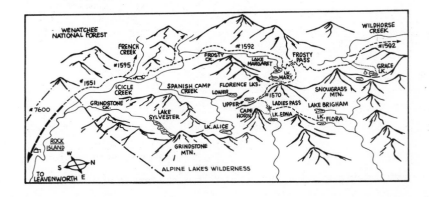

34 LAKE LELAND– SQUARE LAKE

Round trip to Lake Leland 23 miles
Allow 2–3 days
High point 4461 feet
Elevation gain 1600 feet
Hikable mid-July through September
Round trip to Square Lake 23 miles
Allow 2–4 days

High point 5120 feet
Elevation gain 2220 feet
Hikable August through September
Maps: Green Trails No. 176 Stevens Pass and No. 177 Chiwaukum Mountains
Current information: Ask at Leavenworth Ranger Station about trail Nos. 1551, 1566, and 1567

A big bunch of lakes from a single basecamp. This is an unpretentious trip, the sort a hiker luxuriating in lonesomeness might describe as "an ill-favored thing, but mine own." The trail is muddy and brushy, crosses many creeks and windfalls, and scarcely sees a maintenance crew from one decade to the next. Should you persevere you will be rewarded not only by beauty but peace—because there is no easy way. Stoicism can triumph over the ankle-deep mud and head-high brush and the barricades of logs to be crawled over and under. It takes something more, though, to manage the two fords of raging creeks. There's no such thing as a free lunch.

Drive Icicle Creek road (Hike 24) to the end, elevation 2880 feet.

Hike the Icicle Creek trail 6 miles to Bark Camp and Leland Creek

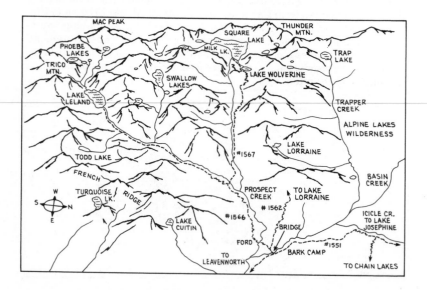

trail No. 1566, 3400 feet (Hike 28). Go left, and cross over Icicle Creek on a large bridge to more camps. In a few hundred feet, the path splits, Lorraine Ridge trail No. 1568 (Hike 35) going right. Go left ¼ mile to a crossing of Leland Creek, if lucky on a logjam. At 8 miles (from the Icicle Creek road) is another split in the trail and a small, comfy camp, ideal for a base to explore both trails.

For Lake Leland follow Leland Creek upstream. At 9¼ miles reach the end of the lower valley, wide and gentle, and enter the narrow and steep upper valley, the briskly climbing trail paralleling a cascad-

Square Lake

ing Leland Creek. At 11½ miles from the road attain Lake Leland, 4461 feet.

Camps are pleasant, the views from the subalpine lake very fine to cliffs of Granite and Trico Mountains, and a goat-nimble hiker can scramble around in steep heather and enjoy views from atop those cliffs. In late summer the outlet stream may be crossed on a logjam to a sketchy trail that climbs 1½ miles to the three Phoebe Lakes, the highest 5214 feet, at the very bottom of Trico's cliffs.

For Square Lake, at the basecamp cross Leland Creek and enter the valley of Prospect Creek. The climb is moderate as far as a series of large avalanche swaths from Thunder Mountain, where the trail is faint and greenery-choked. Just before the first swath, 1¾ miles beyond Leland Creek, is a small camp. Shortly afterward switchbacks begin, starting in brush, continuing in forest.

At 3¼ miles from Leland Creek is the rocky cirque of Lake Wolverine, 5041 feet; no camps here, carry on. The way descends gently in the final ¼ mile to Square Lake, 4989 feet, 11½ miles from the Icicle Creek road. Follow the trail around the shore to the outlet, which was dammed in the remote pre–environmental impact statement passed by Icicle Irrigation District to maintain the flow of Icicle Creek in times of drought. In low water the dam can be crossed with dry feet to an old guard cabin and a very limited camping area.

By poking around a bit, explorers can find little Milk Lake and a second Square Lake, which isn't so square. Goats are suspected of ascending Mac Peak from here and crossing the granite ramparts to Deception Lakes.

35   LAKE LORRAINE

**Round trip to Lake Lorraine 20
   miles**
Allow 2–3 days
High point 5451 feet
**Elevation gain 2700 feet in, 450
   feet out**
Hikable July through September

**Maps: Green Trails No. 176 Stevens
   Pass and No. 177 Chiwaukum
   Mountains**
**Current information: Ask at
   Leavenworth Ranger Station
   about trail Nos. 1551, 1566, and
   1568**

Fill all available canteens and plod straight up a trail built by fire look-
outs who didn't wish to waste time getting to and from work. Sit on the
ground by the site of their long-gone cabin, nibble your blue cheese and
liver sausage, and gaze at peaks and ridges from Icicle Ridge to Stevens
Pass and the topper, Glacier Peak. Then wander along the ridge, sniffing
the flowers, and drop to a small lake with nice camps.

Drive Icicle Creek road (Hike 24) to the end, elevation 2880 feet.

Hike the Icicle Creek and Leland Creek trails 6¼ miles to Lorraine
Ridge trail No. 1568, 3200 feet (Hikes 28 and 34). The hasty trail takes
dead aim up a steep rib to the ridge crest; in ½ mile the rib becomes so ri-
diculously steep that flexing the ankles is a pain, so a few switchbacks are
thrown in. At the end of the sixth switchback, walk out left for a breather
and views up Leland Creek and down Icicle Creek. At 2½ miles (from
Icicle Creek) the twenty-first switchback and forest end at a rock buttress,
the start of a final ½-mile ascent so busy with views that no excuse is
needed for going slow.

Approaching the crest, the trail quits climbing and turns left to contour
along a bench. Spot a faint old path heading uphill right, drop packs, and
in ⅛ mile sit down at the site of the lookout, 5451 feet, a bit below the
summit of Lake Lorraine Point. Get out the maps and spend some time
reciting the names of the peaks you see, such as Bulls Tooth to the west,
Cowboy Mountain north, Mac Peak southwest.

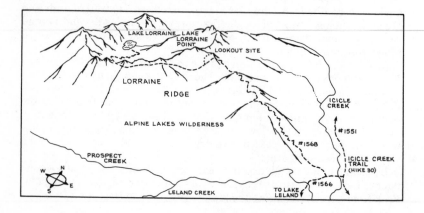

Returned to the packs, continue ½ mile along the trail, near and on the ridge crest, and descend 450 feet to small camps at Lake Lorraine, 5056 feet, 4 miles from the Icicle Creek trail, 10 from the Icicle Creek road.

The ridge path proceeds on the crest, faintly, beaten out by goat hooves, and circles above the lake to a viewpoint above Trapper Creek. The goats probably also have a route to Thunder Mountain Lakes, but that's their business.

Icicle Creek valley from Lorraine Ridge

37 MISSION RIDGE

Round trip to viewpoint 4½ miles
Hiking time 3 hours
High point 3400 feet
Elevation gain 1650 feet
Hikable May through October

One day
Motorcycle country
Map: Use Wenatchee National Forest map
Current information: Ask at Leavenworth Ranger Station about trail No. 1201

The subrange of the Cascades known as the Wenatchee Mountains lies east of the crest in the sunshine country, the land of pine trees and several times the number of flower species at comparable elevations west of the crest. The knife-edge of Mission Ridge samples the open forests and brilliant little meadows, and the fine views as well: down sheer cliffs to Devils Gulch and its weird pinnacles, up to Mission Peak, west to Tronsen Ridge and east to Horselake Mountains, and the scenic climaxes, the craggy-snowy Stuart Range to the west and, to the east, a broad expanse of rolling hills lowering to the infinite flatness of the Columbia Plateau.

But just as a cosmos that has only a Heaven is incomplete and must have a Hell, all this lovely land has been "released" to wheels, one entire geographical–ecological province in which quiet is a rare possibility, where every valley and hill that can be motorcycled is motorcycled. The trail here described was once well graded with switchbacks for hikers and horses; now it's a straight up-and-down wheel chute that year by year is a steadily deepening trench. By coming in midweek in late spring, when snowfields linger, a hiker may be permitted to enjoy the flowers and views in peace, but for months at a time no rational hiker or horse-rider ventures to the blighted gardens. This trail was selected for representation because it is rated the most difficult in the area, so most wheel-jockeys avoid it.

Drive Mission Creek road to the fork at pavement's end (Hike 36). Go left 2.7 miles to the trailhead parking turnout, elevation 1750 feet.

The trail begins on a bridge over East Mission Creek to a fork. Devils

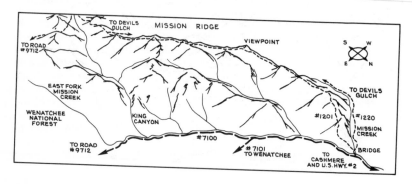

Gulch trail No. 1220 goes right (Hike 38). Go left on Mission Ridge trail No. 1201 and start climbing. After the first switchback the way passes by the first rocky pinnacle and opens out to vistas. The ascent is mainly in the shade of pine trees, yet by a summer noon warm enough. Beyond the rocky first mile, the ridge broadens and the forest floor becomes grassy to an old skid road at 2 miles. In another ¼ mile the ridge changes character again, reverting to rockiness. The lupine is especially lovely from late June to mid-July; in a warm afternoon the perfume may drug you to sleep the way it did the lotus-eaters visited by Odysseus.

At 2½ miles the trail crests a small knoll. Go right on a rough footpath to a jutting rib, a superb viewpoint and a good spot to sit and drink your Gookinaid and eat your bagels and cream cheese. From this knoll the trail takes a deep dip before climbing the next. At 6 miles it passes a group of large rock pinnacles where a tree 10 feet in diameter picturesquely grows from naked rock. At 7½ miles is the high point of the route, 4800 feet, followed by a steep drop to meet the Devils Gulch trail (a loop!) at 8 miles, 4420 feet. From the junction the trail proceeds 2 more miles to the Liberty–Beehive road, a popular trip for motorcycles—bah, humbug.

Mission Ridge

38 DEVILS GULCH

Round trip to last water 15 miles
Hiking time 7 hours
High point 3500 feet
Elevation gain 1750 feet
Hikable May through October
One day or backpack
Loop trip to Mission Ridge 17 miles
Hiking time 10 hours
High point 4800 feet

Elevation gain 3050 feet
Hikable June through October
One day or backpack
Motorcycle country
Map: Use Wenatchee National Forest map
Current information: Ask at Leavenworth Ranger Station about trail Nos. 1201 and 1220

Travelers of olden days were reminded of the Devil by the narrow slot of the valley and the sheer cliffs of its steep walls, the unearthly pinnacles, and the scorching sun of summer. Hikers of today are reminded of Hell as they listen to motorcycles whining and snarling their paean to the Lord of the Flies. However, the good Creation cannot be abandoned to evil. By visiting in late spring or early summer, especially in the middle of the week, a hiker can savor the beauty of the flowers and enjoy the handi-

Lupine beside Devils Gulch trail

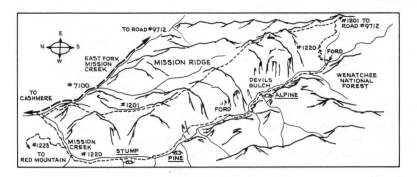

work of the Devil (in the Manichean heresy said to be the Creator), so benign by comparison with His human imps.

Drive Mission Creek road to the fork at pavement's end (Hike 36). Go left 2.7 miles to the trailhead parking turnout, elevation 1750 feet.

Cross East Mission Creek on a plank bridge to a fork. Mission Ridge trail No. 1201 goes left (Hike 36). Go right on Devils Gulch trail No. 1220 and cross Mission Creek.

The trail is maintained (with the money that you, the hiker, pays in gas taxes) for motorcycle convenience and has been rebuilt to let them razz as fast as possible, so look sharp and at blind corners honk your horn. After a single switchback the path begins a long traverse across a slope of rockslides and sheer cliffs interspersed with bands of forest. Note the abundance of animal signs and game traces. At ¹/₂ mile pass a sidetrail up Red Hill, a popular motocross area (Hike 36). Stump Camp, 2¹/₄ miles, 2240 feet, is the first of three maintained campgrounds, should you take your chances on getting any sleep hereabouts, where machines roar by day and beer-drinkers by night.

In ¹/₄ mile the trail crosses Mission Creek on a bridge built for wheels and makes a quick climb from forest back to the steep and open slopes of the gulch, colored in early July by wild roses. At 3 miles, 2360 feet, is Pine Camp; an old bridge serves as a large picnic table, a distinctive touch.

The next crossing of Mission Creek is at 4¹/₂ miles. At 6 miles, beside a small tributary to Mission Creek, is Alpine Camp, 3000 feet.

The path contours hillsides to the final crossing of Mission Creek, 7¹/₂ miles, 3500 feet, a good turnaround for hikers not wishing to loop on over Mission Ridge and, for those who do, the last place to find water.

Switchbacks ascend 1¹/₂ miles to the crest of Mission Ridge and an intersection with Mission Ridge trail, 4420 feet. To complete the loop turn left (Hike 37).

39   INGALLS CREEK

Round trip to Falls Creek Camp
   12 miles
Hiking time 6 hours
High point 3200 feet
Elevation gain 1200 feet
Hikable late May through
   October
One day or backpack
Round trip to Stuart Pass 32
   miles

Allow 3–5 days
High point 6400 feet
Elevation gain 4400 feet
Hikable July through September
Maps: Green Trails No. 209 Mount
   Stuart and No. 210 Liberty
Current information: Ask at
   Leavenworth Ranger Station
   about trail No. 1215

The longest wilderness valley remaining in the Cascades outside the far north, 16 miles of trail climbing from low forest to high meadows passing constantly changing views of the spectacular Stuart Range. Hike this trail the first week of June, when the first 5 miles are lined with trillium, gold-colored paintbrush, and a few calypso orchids thrown in. If you're too early for trillium, there will be glacier lilies. If you're too late for trillium, there will be queen's cup.

Drive US 97 to 12.5 miles north from Swauk (Blewett) Pass and turn left on Ingalls Creek road about 1 mile to the road-end and trailhead, elevation 1953 feet.

The trail ascends steadily but gently, alternating between groves of trees and patches of avalanche brush, mostly in sight and always in sound of roaring Ingalls Creek, with tantalizing glimpses of the rocky summits of the Stuart Range, and later, looks to fantastic spires.

In early June hikers usually will encounter snowpatches from 4 miles or so and difficult going beyond the vicinity of Falls Creek, 6 miles, 3200 feet. The lovely Falls Creek Camp is reached by a sidetrail across Ingalls Creek, which is much too deep and swift to ford while meltwater is rushing. In any season this point makes a good turnaround for day-trippers.

The way continues upward along the almost-straight fault-line valley

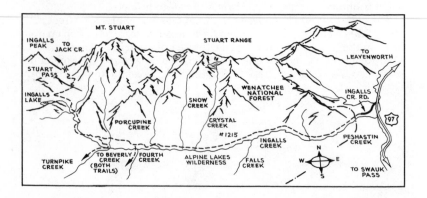

Ingalls Creek

(granite on one side, sediments and metamorphics on the other), the forest becoming subalpine and open, the views growing. Tributary creeks are crossed often; pleasant camps are frequent.

From Porcupine Creek, about 10 miles, 4100 feet, the path steepens a bit and sidehills above Ingalls Creek, the timber increasingly broken by meadows. Now the cliffs and buttresses of 9415-foot Mt. Stuart, second highest nonvolcanic peak in the state, dominate the scene.

At about 13½ miles, 4800 feet, the trail nears Ingalls Creek and commences a rather earnest ascent, climbing parkland and flowers and talus to Stuart Pass, 16 miles, 6400 feet. On the far side the tread descends Jack Creek to Icicle Creek.

All along the upper valley, the open country invites wanderings on sidetrails, such as Longs Pass (Hike 56). From a camp in the delightful basin under Stuart Pass, one can spend days exploring—begin by contouring from the pass to 6463-foot Ingalls Lake (Hike 55).

40 MOUNT LILLIAN LOOPS

Short loop trip 7 miles
Hiking time 4 hours
High point 6000 feet
Elevation gain 400 feet
Hikable late June through
  September
One day or backpack
Long loop trip 11¼ miles
Hiking time 6 hours
High point 6000 feet

Elevation gain 800 feet
Hikable late June through
  September
One day or backpack
Motorcycle country
Map: Green Trails No. 210 Liberty
Current information: Ask at
  Leavenworth Ranger Station
  about trail No. 1204

A short loop hike traverses varied terrain of forest and meadow and ever-changing scenery of the Wenatchee Mountains. A longer loop gives the same but a lot more of it, the more exciting for secluded meadows, striking viewpoints, and numerous sidetrails to explore. (A happy note: This trail is closed to wheels until June 15, giving a chance to do the hike when flowers are best.)

Drive US 97 to Swauk Pass and turn south on road No. 9716, following "Table Mountain" signs. In 3.8 miles go left on road No. 9712 another 4.9 miles to Haney Meadow. To do the long loop, park at the campground, elevation 5502 feet. For the short loop park 0.2 mile farther along on the Old Ellensburg Trail, at 5480 feet.

Short loop: hike road No. 9712 for ¾ mile from the Old Ellensburg Trail to Tiptop–Mt. Lillian trail No. 1204 (Hike 41) and follow it ¼ mile up the valley to an unmarked junction. Go right on a heavily traveled (wheels and all) trail heading rapidly uphill. At 1¾ miles pass a remarkable viewpoint down cliffs to Devils Gulch, 3000 feet below, and out northeast to a sparkle of the Columbia River.

Ascend a knoll and plunge past rocky pinnacles, the trail churned by

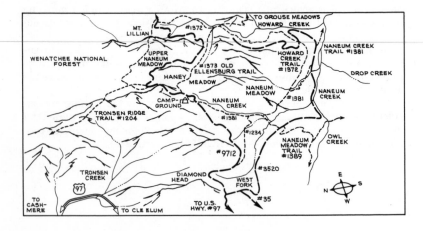

Overlooking Devils Gulch from a shoulder of Mount Lillian

horses and rutted by wheels, at 2½ miles emerging abruptly on road No. 9712. Walk the road east 1000 feet to Howard Creek trail No. 1372 and descend it through meadows and forest, beside the rippling creek, 1¾ miles to Old Ellensburg Trail No. 1373 and a small camp. Take the Old Ellensburg Trail 2 miles back to Haney Meadow to close the loop.

Long loop: continue down Howard Creek a scant ¼ mile to a junction where Old Ellensburg Trail goes left to Grouse Meadow; go right on Howard Creek trail, which turns sharply right and starts climbing. Scenery soon opens from a grassy ridge; across the deep gorge of Howard Creek can be seen a fine display of columnar basalt.

At 5 miles from Haney Meadow, the trail enters a series of clearcuts. Cross a skid road and continue straight, winding around logs and stumps, following a dry streambed, and contouring the edge of a clearcut. Beware of cows giving you the evil eye, a warning to find some other spot to sit and chew your cud.

Howard Creek joins Naneum Creek and the trail rounds the south corner of the loop, crossing another road, passing numerous vistas over the two creeks and the flat top of Table Mountain to the west. At 8¼ miles from Haney Meadow, Howard Creek trail ends at Naneum Creek trail No. 1381, 5200 feet.

Continue straight on this new name, by several possible camps, gently ascending small meadows. At 9 miles the way suddenly drops in several switchbacks to Naneum Meadow and a junction with Naneum Meadow trail No. 1389, 5200 feet.

Cross the meadow, passing the stock gate, circling cliffs of columnar basalt, crossing a muddy creek. At 9¼ miles the trail passes another stock gate at the upper end of the meadow; here is Naneum Camp, a comfortable spot.

Naneum Rim trail branches left; continue straight along Naneum Creek to road No. 9712, reached at 11 miles from the loop start. Cross the road and a small rib to return to Haney Meadow Campground, 11¼ miles.

41 TRONSEN RIDGE

**Round trip to Red Hill trail 8
miles**
Hiking time 5 hours
High point 5840 feet
**Elevation gain 240 feet in, 970
feet out**
**Hikable mid-June through
September**

One day
Motorcycle country
Map: Green Trails No. 210 Liberty
**Current information: Ask at
Leavenworth Ranger Station
about trail No. 1204**

A classic ridge walk over rolling hills of the Wenatchee Mountains
gives splendid views west to snowy peaks of the Cascades and east to
heat-shimmering plains of Columbia River country. An enjoyable hike can
be had by going little more than a mile from the start; the ambitious can
explore another 5 miles beyond the suggested turnaround—chosen because Mt. Adams is visible, a satisfying way to cap the climax.

Drive to Haney Meadow (Hike 40) and 0.9 mile beyond to Tiptop–Mt.
Lillian trail No. 1204 in Upper Naneum Meadow, elevation 5623 feet.
(Don't be confused by the Tronsen Meadow trail—it leads downhill only.)

The first ¼ mile, walk either the trail on the left side of little Naneum
Creek or the road on the right side, the two joining just before Mt. Lillian
trail splits off to the right; stay left on the road. Near the end of the first
mile, it tops a grassy knoll and bends left. Here the ridge trail leaves the
road and drops right, into forest; for a terrific view of the Stuart Range,
Mt. Rainier, and a whole lot else, stay on the road to the end on a rocky
point, then follow a motorcycle rut steeply down to the trail.

The way rolls along the crest of Tronsen Ridge, climbing in short spurts
to summits and falling back down to saddles. Motorcycle fun-tracks shortcut and crisscross; choose the gentlest angle up or down to stay on the real
trail.

At about 3 miles US 970 comes in view when the path dips to the west
side of the ridge to traverse beneath picturesque sandstone spires, a rock
climber's delight. At 3¾ miles pass a wheel shortcut to Red Hill trail No.
1223 (Hike 36) and in ¼ mile more reach the official junction. See Mt.

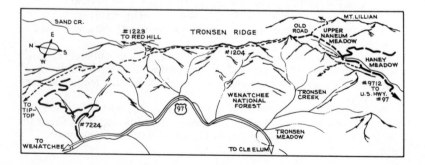

Sandstone cliff on Tronsen Ridge

Adams, kill off the sardines and the root beer, and return.

Or, continue to road No. 7224 at 7 miles, the abandoned West Sand Creek trail at 8 miles, and the end of the ridge trail at Ruby Creek in 9 miles. Study the map and invent loops.

Stuart Range from Three Brothers

SWAUK CREEK
Unprotected area

42 THREE BROTHERS

**Round trip 4 miles plus access 16
  miles**
Hiking time (trail only) 3 hours
High point 7169 feet
Elevation gain 2139 feet
**Hikable mid-July through
  September**

One day plus access
Motorcycle country
**Maps: Green Trails No. 209 Mount
  Stuart and No. 210 Liberty**
**Current information: Ask at
  Leavenworth Ranger Station
  about trail No. 1211**

In an age of crowded wilderness, backcountry overuse, and the conse-
quent need for rationing-by-permits, the Three Brothers trail is like a
time-travel trip back to the Golden Age. The path is in good condition, the
meadows are colorful, the views outstanding—and people are few. There
is a catch: access to the trailhead is across private land in the Negro
Creek valley, with the only vehicles allowed being those of workers or
residents.

Three approaches may be made to the Three Brothers trail. The most
scenic is via Ingalls Creek, a 12½-mile route with an elevation gain of
4400 feet. Follow Ingalls Creek trail (Hike 39) 5½ miles and then ascend
Falls Creek trail to a 6100-foot pass. Descend trail No. 1210 to its end at
an unmarked road. Go left, an uphill mile. Leave the road 100 feet after it
dips and crosses Gold Creek. Bushwhack up 150 feet to intersect the old

114

trail. (The actual trailhead lies another ½ mile *down* the road in an old clearcut.)

The alternate approach is 10 miles via Negro Creek valley. Carry a good map and be prepared for bushwhacking, 10 creek crossings that should be attempted only in late summer or fall when the creek is low, and an elevation gain of 3100 feet. The hike begins at the Ingalls Creek trailhead and follows the old Blewett Pass Highway, paralleling US 97. At 2 miles the road turns up Negro Creek and passes a series of very messy prospecting operations. At 4½ miles the road is washed out, and what's left of the old grade has degenerated to a rough and brushy trail. When this ends at a miner's cabin at 6½ miles, go right on a well-maintained road. At 8 miles the Iron Mountain road joins on the left and ½ mile beyond this junction the road splits. Go right, cross Negro Creek, and follow "Trail" signs ¼ mile to trail No. 1210, described in the above paragraph.

The third approach is a gated road from Shaser Creek, over Iron Mountain, and down into the Negro Creek drainage. Drive US 97 north from Swauk (Blewett) Pass 6.8 miles to the Scotty Creek–Old Blewett Pass turnoff. Head up road No. 7320 for 0.8 mile and turn right on road No. 7322 for 0.5 miles to a large intersection. Vehicles with low clearance should park here. Take the road on the right and head up the North Shaser Creek valley 1¼ miles to road No. 400, which is gated. Go right, climbing steeply 3 miles to the crest of Iron Mountain, and descend 2½ miles into the Negro Creek valley. At the bottom of the descent go left ½ mile to a second intersection and turn right. Cross Negro Creek to another intersection and take a left. In ¼ mile pass trail No. 1210. Follow directions as noted above. This access is 8 miles long with an elevation gain of 3200 feet and a loss of 900 feet.

The Three Brothers trail climbs steadily through Gold Basin, at 1¼ miles passing an old mine to the right and an old cabin foundation on the left. This foundation is an excellent tent platform, though late in the season the camp may be dry. Near the top of the Middle Brother, Mt. Rainier, Mt. Adams, and the Wenatchee Mountains come in view. At the crest is a magnificent panorama of the Stuart Range.

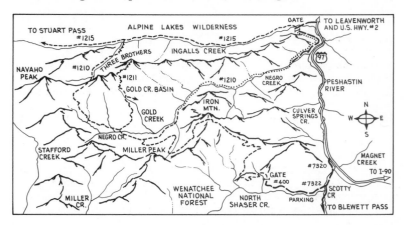

Blewett Ridge trail

SWAUK CREEK
Unprotected area

43   BLEWETT RIDGE

Round trip to Miller Peak 10½ miles
Hiking time 7 hours
High point 6400 feet
Elevation gain 1700 feet plus ups and downs
Hikable July through mid-October

One day
Motorcycle country
Map: Green Trails No. 210 Liberty
Current information: Ask at Cle Elum Ranger Station about trail No. 1226

Airy meadows of the narrow crest look out to the Wenatchee Mountains, pure motorcycle country, and high ice and rock of the Stuart Range, pure wilderness. Blewett Ridge is the nearest thing to a wilderness experience possible in a locality dissected by public and private logging operations, largely because though the trail has been partly rebuilt—on the National Forest sections only—to let motorcycles run fast and loose, the starting point is so obscure it rarely receives any use whatsoever.

Part of the County Line Trail (Hike 49), the Blewett Ridge trail starts at Blewett Pass. The early stretch, however, is very brushy and hard to follow, so a beginning a mile or so along the old route is described here. Getting to it is no cinch because the logging roads are mostly private and unmaintained and have no numbers or signs. Your car may suggest that you walk all or some of the road distance from Blewett Pass, elevation 4064 feet.

Drive US 97 north 3.2 miles from Mineral Spring Resort or 4.8 miles west from Swauk Pass and take the Old Blewett Road 3.8 miles to Blewett Pass. At the summit turn left, steeply uphill, on a very poor private road. In 0.2 mile turn left at the first junction and at 0.5 mile left again, sidehilling downward. At the bottom take a very hard left. In 2000 feet go right 0.7 mile, crossing the crest of Blewett Ridge and dropping. At the bottom look left to spot the unmarked trailhead, elevation 4700 feet.

The trail climbs steadily the first mile to gain the 5440-foot summit of the ridge's first attainment of mile-high elevation. Near the top the path is cut by a logging road; head straight up from the last recognizable portion of trail to find it again.

The big views begin as the route waltzes along the crest from summit to summit, switching from side to side. A steep descent of woods and ascent of a field of grass lead to Teanaway Ridge trail No. 1364 (Hike 44). Proceed onward, dropping to a clearcut in a saddle and beginning the climb of open meadows to Miller Peak.

At 4 miles the trail quits the ridge for a long contour around Miller Peak to new views of Navaho Peak and Mt. Stuart. At 5 miles, 5600 feet, join the Miller Peak trail (Hike 46) for the final ¼-mile push to the summit, 6402 feet, which might logically be considered the terminus of Blewett Ridge, though the divide goes on to more peaks.

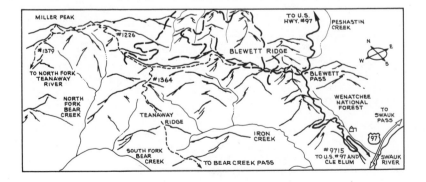

44 IRON CREEK– TEANAWAY RIDGE

Round trip to 5489-foot knoll 6
miles
Hiking time 4 hours
High point 5489 feet
Elevation gain 1900 feet
Hikable mid-June through mid-
October

One day
Motorcycle country
Map: Green Trails No. 210 Liberty
Current information: Ask at Cle
Elum Ranger Station about trail
Nos. 1351 and 1364

A relatively short climb (but dry—carry loaded canteens) yields rich dividends of meadows and views—nearby to the Stuart Range, far away to Rainier. Once the ridge is attained, the highline rambling can go for miles, in several directions. Sorry to say—as must be done so often in the east-slope Cascades—it's motorcycle country, the trails rebuilt (not "improved") for speedy wheeling. Until this madness is halted, the hike is best done midweek, when there is some chance of being able to hear birdsongs and bumblebee buzzes.

Drive US 97 north 2.3 miles from Mineral Spring Resort or 5.7 miles west from Swauk Pass and make a sharp turn west off the highway and immediately north onto Iron Creek road No. 9714. In 3.6 miles are the road-end and Iron Creek–Bear Creek trail No. 1351, elevation 3600 feet.

The trail sets out steeply up the barren, rubbly slopes characteristic of this area—in late spring through the anomalous exuberance of flowers that are also characteristic. At 1 mile attain Iron Creek–Bear Creek Pass, 4480 feet, and a four-way stop. The straight-ahead trail drops 3½ miles down Bear Creek to road No. 9738. Teanaway Ridge trail No. 1364 goes left 3½ up-and-down miles to road No. (9702)120. Turn right on a new section of the latter trail, the route to the high country.

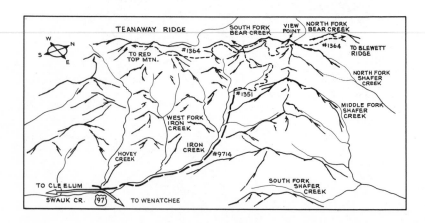

Mount Stuart and Miller Peak from Teanaway Ridge

The way ascends the narrow and rocky crest of the ridge, then traverses long switchbacks up an ancient burn, views expanding by the step, at 3 miles from the road topping out on a 5489-foot knoll, a great place to get out the maps and the granola bars and the chocolate-chip cookies. Miller Peak is only 1½ air miles distant, the snow-patched and granite-walled crags of the Stuart Range beyond; Stuart is seen from here as a sharp-cleavered triangular peak notably higher than its neighbors. Tronsen Ridge is east. South looms the big white mound of Mt. Rainier.

For the information of ridgerunners, from here the trail drops 300 feet and at 4 miles climbs to the Blewett Ridge segment of County Line trail No. 1226, which leads in either direction through flowers and views (Hike 43).

45   NAVAHO PASS

Round trip 11 miles
Hiking time 5 hours
High point 6000 feet
Elevation gain 2000 feet
Hikable mid-June through
   September

One day or backpack
Map: Green Trails No. 209 Mount
   Stuart
Current information: Ask at Cle
   Elum Ranger Station about trail
   No. 1359

Hike close along a babbling-burbling stream, passing many nice camps, climbing quite steeply, and clambering over a few logs (the better to discourage the wheel-freaks), up through brilliant dry-climate gardens to a high pass with stupendous views across Ingalls Creek to the Stuart Range.

Drive US 970 north 5 miles from Interstate 90 and turn west on Teanaway River road. Follow "North Fork Teanaway" signs 13.5 miles to a major junction at 29 Pines Campground. Go right 1.3 miles on road No. 9737, then right on Stafford Creek road No. 9707, in 2.5 miles crossing Stafford Creek to Stafford Creek trail No. 1359, elevation 3100 feet.

The trail starts on an old jeep track, quickly narrows to the real thing, and climbs steadily but rarely steeply, sometimes beside the creek and other times a stone's throw above. The first 2 miles are through tall pine, hemlock, and silver fir. These thin out, yielding to the little dry-and-stony meadows typical of the area, the plants sparse but in early summer blooming in all colors of the rainbow.

At 4 miles, 5100 feet, is a junction with Standup Creek trail No. 1369. Confusingly, the trail signs imply that Stafford Creek trail becomes Standup Creek trail. Whatever, go right, following the sign pointing to "Negro Creek trail 1 mile"; be prepared for 1½ or 2 miles. The way makes a long switchback with downvalley views, then climbs in short switchbacks to a pass just west of Navaho Peak and thus here dubbed "Navaho Pass," 5½ miles, 6100 feet.

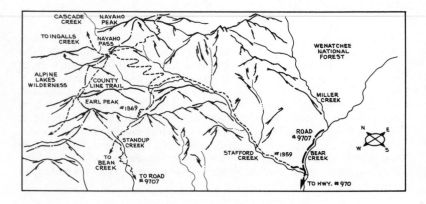

The pass is on the boundary of the Alpine Lakes Wilderness, which encompasses the deep gulf of Ingalls Creek beneath and the high-leaping wall of the Stuart Range beyond. Mt. Stuart itself is cut off from view, but Little Annapurna and 8364-foot McClellan Peak are most acceptable stand-ins.

At the pass is a four-way intersection. Cascade Creek trail drops 5 miles to Ingalls Creek. To the east, the slopes of 7223-foot Navaho Peak are traversed by Negro Creek trail, whose name reminds that not all pioneers were of European descent. (The original name, as late as the 1960s used on government maps, was the racial epithet used by the miners. The government very properly has amended its maps but in so doing substituted a term once considered polite but now felt by most Americans of African descent to be as demeaning as the older epithet.) To the west the County Line Trail, less a real trail (Hike 49) than a figment of the memory, follows the ridge crest a ways, contours around a high point, and drops to Hardscrabble Creek basin.

Mount Stuart Range from Navaho Pass

Balsamroot on Miller Peak

NORTH FORK TEANAWAY RIVER
Unprotected area

46   MILLER PEAK

Round trip 9 miles
Hiking time 5 hours
High point 6400 feet
Elevation gain 3200 feet
Hikable July through September
One day

Motorcycle country
Maps: Green Trails No. 209 Mount
    Stuart and No. 210 Liberty
Current information: Ask at Cle
    Elum Ranger Station about trail
    No. 1379

A glorious viewpoint of the dark massif of the Stuart Range, the arid-brown Wenatchee Range overlooking Swauk and Blewett Passes, the huge whiteness of Mt. Rainier and Mt. Adams, and much greenery amid the rocks of nearby Navaho Peak, Three Brothers, and Iron Mountain.

Drive Stafford Creek road (Hike 45) 3.5 miles to the end at the confluence of Miller and Bear Creeks and the parking lot for their trails, elevation 3200 feet.

Miller Creek boasts another of the motorcycle expressways that plague the area, but in midweek when the wheels are away the hikers can play, far more quietly. The trail starts on the west side of the creek but soon switches to the east. On this crossing and the several that follow, logjams and boulders must serve as footbridges.

A gentle ascent 2 miles along the creek brings the valley end. Gaze far above to green meadows and think what a haul the getting there must be. It is. Switchbacks handsomely graded for wheels climb and climb, at 3½ miles, 5200 feet, attaining a saddle in the ridge jutting from Miller Peak between Miller and Bear Creek valleys. Here are the first broad views.

The way traverses the west side of the ridge over steep, green meadows to meet the County Line Trail (Hikes 43 and 49) at 4 miles; the camp at the junction has no water after the snows melt. A final ¼ mile switchbacks to a saddle 300 feet below the summit, the stopping place of trail and motorcycles. A meager bootpath completes the ascent of the rock summit, cliffs on three sides, too airy for most folks to enjoy on a foggy day, and some in sunshine. From the peak or the trail's end, views will keep your head swinging from side to side almost too fast for your carrot sticks and celery stalks to find your mouth.

To the south along Blewett Ridge (Hike 43) the County Line Trail is groomed for motorcycles, suggesting to a hiker equipped with ice ax the advantages of visiting in June, when snowfields keep the peace. For a loop, follow this trail to the Iron Creek–Bear Creek trail, the return to the parking lot; 12¾ miles, a nice day. Experienced wildland navigators can have good sport trying to follow the County Line Trail north; not maintained and through the meadows never even built, the route is notably uncrowded.

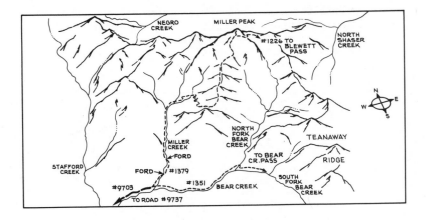

47   BEAN CREEK BASIN

**Round trip to upper basin
  5 miles
Hiking time 3½ hours
High point 5500 feet
Elevation gain 1900 feet
Hikable mid-June through mid-
  October**

**One day
Map: Green Trails No. 209 Mount
  Stuart
Current information: Ask at Cle
  Elum Ranger Station about trail
  Nos. 1391 and 1391A**

What's your pleasure? Views to Mt. Stuart and the Columbia Plateau? These are to be had by climbing above Bean Creek Basin to the ridge tops. Or are you content with wet meadows where the monkeyflower and willow herb bloom and with dry meadows of the buckwheat and skyrocket gilia? If so, the basin floor is your game.

Drive the North Fork Teanaway road No. 9737 (Hike 45) 16.5 miles to Beverly Creek. Just before crossing the creek, turn right 0.7 mile on the Beverly Creek road No. (9737)112 to the washed-out bridge, elevation 3400 feet.

Follow the abandoned road ½ mile to the road-end and Beverly–Turnpike trail No. 1391, the first ½ mile on old logging road through clearcuts. Just before the unbridged crossing of Bean Creek, turn right on Bean Creek trail No. 1391A, which soon leaves logged land for forest and begins a relentless, steep ascent of the valley. At ¾ mile cross Bean Creek—easily on boulders in late summer but with wet feet and hips while the snowmelt is rushing, this unfortunately coinciding with the time of richest blooming.

Alternating between bright mountain gardens and cool mountain forests, the way comes to the lower basin and a split in the trail at 2 miles, 5000 feet. Here you must choose your pleasure.

The left fork climbs into Bean Creek Basin. For sensational views, turn

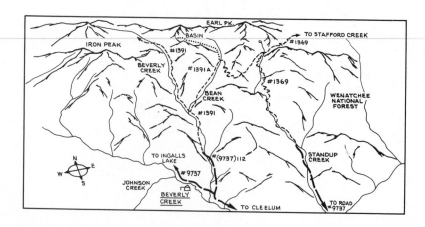

Field of eriogonum in Bean Creek Basin

right on Bean Creek trail and climb 1½ miles to a 6150-foot shoulder southwest of Earl Peak and continue ½ mile, joining the Standup Creek trail, to a 5888-foot saddle on the southeast ridge of Earl. This section of trail is rarely used and poorly defined, especially in meadows; the occasional cairn helps.

From the 5100-foot junction in Bean Creek valley, the basin trail forges resolutely forward a couple of hundred feet and abruptly dies. Continue along faint bootpaths on either side of the creek ½ mile to lush meadows of the upper basin, 5600 feet.

For flowers of the dry meadows proceed up the basin as it bends west, leaving trees behind. For views to top off the trip, climb to the ridge at 6400 feet, and from the boundary of the Alpine Lakes Wilderness look the Stuart Range right in the face, as well as Earl and Iron Peaks and Beverly and Ingalls Creeks.

48 BEVERLY–TURNPIKE

Round trip to Ingalls Creek 16
  miles
Allow 2 days
High point 5800 feet
Elevation gain 2400 feet in, 1000
  feet out
Hikable mid-July through mid-
  October

Maps: Green Trails No. 209 Mount
  Stuart and No. 210 Liberty
Current information: Ask at Cle
  Elum Ranger Station about trail
  No. 1391

Cross a high pass from the Teanaway River valley to Ingalls Creek.
Climb through open forests, flower fields, rock gardens, and views, including 9415-foot Mt. Stuart, second-highest nonvolcanic mountain in the
state. In proper season the flowers begin at the trailhead and never quit,
climaxing in the weird, desertlike serpentine barrens for which the area is
famed among botanists. A stream crossing near the start can give trouble
in the high water of early summer.

Drive to the washed-out bridge on Beverly Creek road (Hike 47), elevation 3400 feet.

Walk the abandoned road ½ mile to its end and start of trail No. 1391,
which starts steeply up a clearcut, quickly passes a junction with the
Bean Creek trail (Hike 47), and then faces the high-water challenge, the
crossing of Bean Creek. The trail sidehills high above Beverly Creek on a
rocky hillside, brilliant at the right time with the yellow of buckwheat and
the scarlet of gilia, and at 3 miles meets Fourth Creek trail, a possible alternate return. Beverly Creek is crossed and switchbacks climb to 5800-
foot Beverly–Turnpike Pass, 4 miles.

The north side of the pass is densely forested; for views of Stuart climb
the hill to the left (northwest) of the pass. But the really terrific sidetrip of
this locality takes off just before the pass on the Iron Peak trail (Hike 53)
and leads up to the serpentine barrens and a superb ridgecrest stroll in
crazy rocks and violent flowers and big views down to and across the
Teanaway River.

From the pass the trail drops through woods and switchbacks steeply

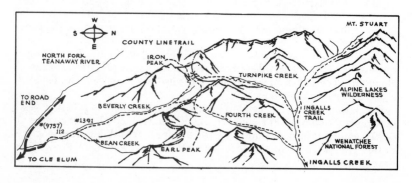

down a barren avalanche slope to the valley bottom and a pleasant forest walk along Turnpike Creek. At 6½ miles, by a nice campsite, is a crossing of the creek (again, possibly difficult). The way then climbs a bit and drops to a crossing of Ingalls Creek—unless a log (scarce) can be found, this is impossible at high water. On the far side is the Ingalls Creek trail (Hike 39). For a loop trip, follow the Ingalls Creek trail downstream 1½ miles to the junction with Fourth Creek trail, recross Ingalls Creek, follow Fourth Creek up to its source, cross the ridge, and rejoin the Beverly–Turnpike trail.

Mount Stuart from Beverly-Turnpike Pass

49 COUNTY LINE TRAIL— FORGOTTEN TRAIL OF THE WENATCHEE MOUNTAINS

The Forgotten Trail
Round trip 16 miles
Hiking time 10 hours
High point 6400 feet
Elevation gain 3500 feet in, 500
feet out
Hikable July through
October
One day
Blewett Pass to Cle Elum River
One way 32 miles

Allow 4–5 days
High point 6400 feet
Elevation gain 4100 feet
Hikable June through October
Maps: Green Trails No. 209 Mount
Stuart and No. 210 Liberty and
USGS Enchantment Lakes
Current information: Ask at Cle
Elum Ranger Station about trail
Nos. 1218 and 1391

The County Line Trail traverses the crest of the Wenatchee Mountains, these being the boundary between two counties, and offers two very different sets of views. On the Chelan County side are the spectacular peaks of the Stuart Range; on the Kittitas County side are foothills and farms.

Cloud-capped Mount Stuart from County Line Trail

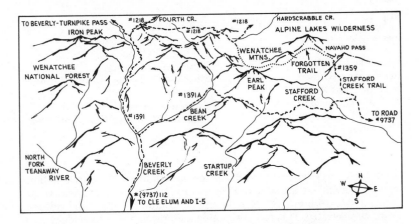

The highlights of the full 32 miles from Blewett Pass to the Cle Elum River are described in Hike 43 (Blewett Ridge) and then, after a 4-mile off-trail ridge walk to Falls Creek trail No. 1216, which is *not* described herein, in Hike 45 (Navaho Pass), Hike 46 (Miller Peak), Hike 48 (Beverly–Turnpike), Hike 53 (Iron Peak), and Hike 54 (Esmerelda Basin), leaving the most spectacular section, the forgotten portion of the County Line Trail, to be described here.

The forgotten 5 miles of trail between Fourth Creek and Stafford Creek were built in the 1920s and abandoned in the 1940s. Bits and pieces can be found but much of the tread has vanished. This part, therefore, is not your usual trail walk but rather a route to be attempted only with aid of maps—USGS, Green Trails, and/or old ones of the Forest Service.

Drive to the Beverly Creek trailhead (Hike 47), elevation 3400 feet.

Hike Beverly Creek trail No. 1391 for 3 miles. Turn right 1 mile on Fourth Creek trail No. 1218 to a 5550-foot pass and the beginning of the Forgotten Trail.

At the pass, trail No. 1218 goes both straight ahead and right. Go right on the seldom-used tread of Hardscrabble Creek trail as it contours high above Ingalls Creek, climbs over a 6400-foot ridge, and drops 400 feet to headwaters of Hardscrabble Creek. At approximately 2 miles from Fourth Creek trail, where the Hardscrabble Creek trail turns sharply downward, is a hard-to-find junction. Stay high and search for remnants of the old tread as it first contours below Earl Peak and then climbs to a 6400-foot shoulder of Earl Peak, 8 miles from the car. Most hikers are content to turn back here.

The sometimes-trail continues another 2 miles, crossing to the Kittitas County side of the ridge to join the Stafford Creek trail (Hike 45) near Navaho Peak.

50 MEDRA PASS

Round trip 8 miles
Hiking time 5 hours
High point 5440 feet
Elevation gain 2340 feet
Hikable July through mid-October
One day

Motorcycle country
Map: Green Trails No. 209 Mount Stuart
Current information: Ask at Cle Elum Ranger Station about trail No. 1383

Follow a pretty creek through the forest awhile, climb rocky and flowery slopes awhile, then sit awhile at Medra Pass and look one way to Mt. Stuart and the other to Mt. Rainier and all around to valleys and ridges of Teanaway country. This is a designated motorcycle trail but seldom used.

Drive the North Fork Teanaway River road (Hike 45) 17.6 miles to Beverly Campground. Continue past the official camp area to an unofficial camp. Park here or in a two-car space at the trailhead (unsigned in 1991), elevation 3100 feet.

Cross the North Fork Teanaway River on a sturdy horse bridge and wind along narrow Johnson Creek valley ¾ mile to a split in the trail. Trail No. 1383.1 goes left up South Fork Johnson Creek and over a wooded, 4500-foot ridge to Jungle Creek. Go right on trail No. 1383 up North Fork Johnson Creek, the forest broken by fields of brush. The path switches from the east side of the creek to the west, recrosses, and repeats the flip-flop in less than ½ mile; early-season hikers might keep drier feet by staying on the east side.

At 2¼ miles a switchback signals the end of water and a change in strategy. The way climbs the valley wall, leaving woods for opens, at 3½ miles attaining the top of the ridge. Views include the North Fork Teanaway valley below and, beyond, Mt. Stuart and the needle-crested Stuart Range. To these at Medra Pass, 4 miles, 5440 feet, are added the

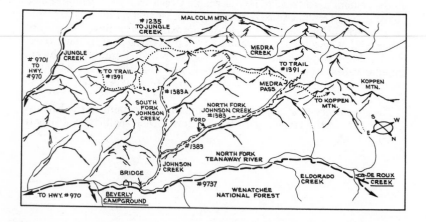

Mount Rainier from Medra Pass

Middle Fork Teanaway valley and, seeming to be just over the next ridge, the gleaming slopes of Mt. Rainier.

The trail, very faint now, continues 2¼ miles down Medra Creek to the Middle Fork trail. However, if more exercise than attaining the pass is wanted, the best views are north and south along the ridge crest. North 2 miles is Koppen Mountain (Hike 52). South the path wanders the tops 4 miles to join trail No. 1383, a loop return—if you're lucky—to where you came from.

51   GALLAGHER HEAD LAKE

**Round trip to Gallagher Head
Lake 8 miles**
Hiking time 5 hours
High point 5600 feet
Elevation gain 1800 feet
**Hikable late June through
October**
One day or backpack
**Loop trip around Esmerelda
Basin 15 miles**
Hiking time 10 hours

High point 5600 feet
Elevation gain 3000 feet
Hikable July through October
One day or backpack
ORV country
**Map: Green Trails No. 209 Mount
Stuart**
**Current information: Ask at Cle
Elum Ranger Station about trail
No. 1392**

Ascend a forest trail to a valley of green meadows and a lazy stream feeding a marsh-lake beneath the crags of Esmerelda Peak and the rounder profiles of Hawkins Mountain and Gallagher Head Mountain. Paradise enow? Indeed. Yet the Forest Service allows jeeps to maraud through Heaven on an abandoned mining track.

Drive North Fork Teanaway River road (Hike 45) 22.1 miles and turn left on a road signed "Trail 1392." In 0.3 mile, near the far end of semi-abandoned De Roux Campground, find unsigned Boulder–De Roux trail No. 1392, elevation 3800 feet.

The trail is heavily traveled by horses and alternates between stretches that have been pounded to powdery sand and others that are ankle-twisting rocky and nose-twisting smelly. Don't complain too loud because the horse damage is a major reason there are no motorcycles.

In a scant ¼ mile cross the North Fork Teanaway; if the bridge is gone hope for a log. After ¾ forested mile cross De Roux Creek on a log and shortly come to a split in the trail, 4100 feet. The left fork is De Roux spur

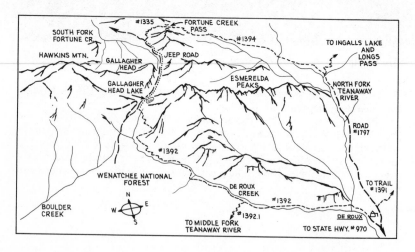

No. 1392.1 signed "Middle Fork Teanaway–Koppen Mountain Trail" (Hike 52). Keep right along the creek, the way steepening to gain 800 feet in the next long mile along a spectacular slot-gorge of De Roux Creek where the rocks, in season, are a pink glow of lewisia blossoms. The way gentles out in grade and at about 2¼ miles walks a log over the creek, here quietly meandering, and enters a meadowy vale offering numerous campsites, 5000 feet. At the upper end of the ½-mile-long valley, the trail turns upward in a series of switchbacks. Across the valley are bright orange cliffs of a nameless ridge and a view south to Koppen Peak. At 4 miles the climbing ends in meadows ringing Gallagher Head Lake, the flower fields rutted by fun wheels from the Fortune Creek jeep road.

For a 15-mile loop, follow the jeep track northward 1 mile, losing 450 feet. Turn right on trail No. 1335 and climb a scant 1000 feet to Fortune Creek Pass. Go right on Esmerelda Basin trail No. 1394 and descend 3½ miles to the North Fork Teanaway River Road (Hike 54). Walk the road 1½ miles to the Boulder–De Roux trailhead. On a survey in late July, more than 150 species of flowers were in bloom on this route.

Gallagher Head Lake

Koppen Mountain trail

52   KOPPEN MOUNTAIN

Round trip 7 miles
Hiking time 4 hours
High point 6031 feet
Elevation gain 2331 feet
Hikable July through
   September

One day
Map: Green Trails No. 209 Mount
   Stuart
Current information: Ask at Cle
   Elum Ranger Station about trail
   No. 1392.1

Look west over the Middle Fork Teanaway valley to meadowy ridges dominated by Jolly Mountain, then turn around and take a single step east (the summit of Koppen Mountain is not large) and gaze over the North Fork Teanaway valley to the massif of Mt. Stuart and lesser foreground peaks, Iron and Esmerelda.

Drive North Fork Teanaway River road to Boulder–De Roux trail No. 1392 (Hike 51). Hike the trail ¾ mile to a junction. The Boulder–De Roux trail climbs right, to Gallagher Head Lake and points beyond. Go left on Middle Fork Teanaway spur trail No. 1392.1, ascending forest, then meadows, to the ridge top, 5100 feet, 1½ miles from the split. Turn left on the unmarked Koppen Mountain trail, built in the 1930s when the mountain was an observation point for fire patrols. The trail is now rough and poorly defined through green meadows and scree slopes of bluish green serpentine.

Views to the left of you, views to the right of you. Those of Mt. Stuart framed by twisted old snags are breathtaking. At 3½ miles from the road, a final push reaches the summit of Koppen Mountain, 6031 feet.

It's been such a relaxing morning that after all the rye wafers and truffled pate are gone a person might wish to wander on along the ridgetop trail toward Medra Pass (Hike 50), 2 miles distant.

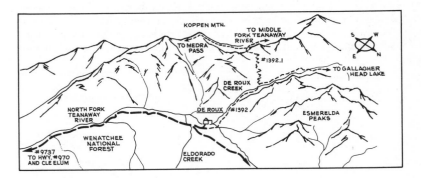

53   IRON PEAK

Round trip to saddle 5 miles
Hiking time 4 hours
High point 6100 feet
Elevation gain 2590 feet
Hikable mid-July through
  September

One day
Map: Green Trails No. 209 Mount
  Stuart
Current information: Ask at Cle
  Elum Ranger Station about trail
  No. 1399

If you want the Teanaway's biggest bang for the buck, view-wise and energy-wise, switchback up and up a long-abandoned stock trail reopened in 1977 by the Youth Conservation Corps. The views start at the car and never quit. In early summer the same is true of the flowers.

Drive North Fork Teanaway River road (Hike 45) 22.6 miles from US 970 and park at the Iron Creek crossing, elevation 3920 feet.

The trail is all switchbacks, zigging-zagging back and forth across a rounded rib between Iron Creek on the left and Eldorado Creek on the right, usually in sound of the water but never in reach, so fill the canteens before setting out. The views, initially across the Teanaway valley to the gorge of De Roux Creek, soon grow to include Koppen Mountain and Esmerelda Peaks. In early summer, though, the eyes may never be raised from the ground, for the open forest and the open screes nourish such an assortment of buckwheats and desert parsleys and orange-and-yellow paintbrushes as a Puget Sounder never dreamt of in his botany.

The rib fades into the hillside and the trail crosses the meadow headwaters (dry) of Eldorado Creek to a rocky saddle, 6100 feet, at 2½ miles. The trail descends from the saddle ½ mile to the Beverly–Turnpike trail, 5600 feet (Hike 48). Turn right on a boot-beaten path along the spur ridge jutting southerly from the Teanaway–Ingalls divide.

If you've never studied flowers before, start now. Little benches in the side of the ridge hold snow late and feed an exuberance of wet-meadow plants. The serpentine barrens support the merest scattered patches of life, but these include species that grow nowhere except in serpentine soils, bringing botanists from afar to admire the rarities, some found only

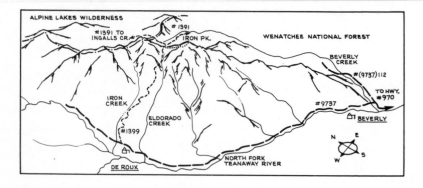

Silver forest high on Iron Peak

in this vicinity. The crazy rocks of the crest are notable for the peculiar seed pods of a very funny sort of crazyweed, as well as violet cushions of douglasia.

As for the views, they comprehend the whole Teanaway region, Mt. Stuart the supreme lord. The bootpath ends on a broad fellfield but the next rise is a simple walk to better views of Stuart. An easy scramble over buttresses and flowers in crannied nooks leads to the summit of Iron Peak, 6510 feet.

54 ESMERELDA BASIN

Round trip to Fortune Creek
  Pass 7 miles
Hiking time 5 hours
High point 6000 feet
Elevation gain 1750 feet
Hikable late June through
  October
One day or backpack
Loop trip around the Esmereldas
  15 miles

Hiking time 10 hours
High point 6000 feet
Elevation gain 3000 feet
Hikable July through October
One day or backpack
Map: Green Trails No. 209 Mount
  Stuart
Current information: Ask at Cle
  Elum Ranger Station about trail
  No. 1394

Pass through a slot between craggy peaks into a secluded basin of forests, streams, and wildflowers the more vivid for contrasting rockslide barrens. Climb to wide views at Fortune Creek Pass. Or cross the pass on a loop trip that completely encircles Esmerelda Peaks. Esmerelda Basin is splendid for day and weekend hikes, particularly when the Cascade Crest is misty-dripping and the sun is (maybe) brilliant here in the rainshadow. Close-to-road camps are ideal for families introducing small children to backpacking.

Drive North Fork Teanaway River road (Hike 45) some 23 miles to its end at the trailhead parking lot, elevation 4243 feet.

The hike starts on a prospecting road built in 1910; modern-day "miners" drive in now and then to play-act their fantasies, and if not for them the scene would be where it belongs—in the Alpine Lakes Wilderness. As it is, the basin is closed to public motor vehicles and the road can be tolerated as merely a wide trail. Ascending within sight and sound of the

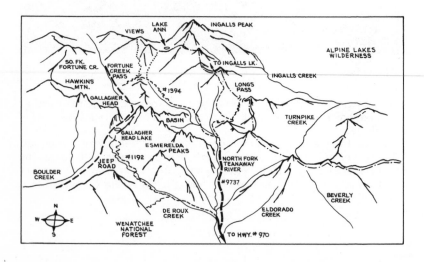

Left, elephanthead; right, columbine

creek-size river, in ¼ mile the old road passes the trail to Ingalls Lake and Longs Pass (Hikes 55 and 56). Soon the way flattens in streamside greenery and rock gardens. Good campsites hereabouts, above and below the road; by late summer this may be the last water of the trip.

The way traverses a rocky avalanche slope, brilliant in late July with scarlet gilia and buckwheat, skirts marshy meadows of pink elephanthead and white bog orchid, and crosses creeks lined by violet shooting stars and blue butterwort.

At 2 miles a modern-built trail diverges from the old mine road and ascends to Fortune Creek Pass, 6000 feet, 3½ miles. For bigger views climb the righthand (north) skyline to a 6500-foot hilltop. Or, drop back down from the pass ¼ mile to the last creek and ascend it to a hidden basin and a pass overlooking Lake Ann, a secret tarn.

For the loop (also described in Hike 51) stay on the main trail, dropping 1000 feet through flower fields to the Fortune Creek jeep road, which the Forest Service stubbornly refuses to close to wheels, thereby permitting the area to be placed in wilderness. Go left 1 mile, gaining 450 feet to Gallagher Head Lake, 4 miles from the DeRoux Creek Campground (Hike 51), 1½ miles from the starting point.

55 INGALLS LAKE

**Round trip to Ingalls Lake
9 miles
Hiking time 8 hours
High point 6500 feet
Elevation gain 2600 feet in, 600
feet out
Hikable mid-July through mid-
October**

**One day or backpack
Map: Green Trails No. 209 Mount
Stuart
Current information: Ask at Cle
Elum Ranger Station about trail
No. 1390**

A rock-basin lake at the foot of rugged Ingalls Peak, at the top of water-falls plunging to Ingalls Creek, and directly across the valley from the massive south wall of 9415-foot Mt. Stuart, the highest peak between Gla-cier and Rainier. The color magic of blue lake, snowfields, ice-polished slabs of brown rock, lush green meadows, a glory of flowers, and groves of whitebark pine, larch, and subalpine fir is purely surreal in the side-lighting of an autumn sunset.

Drive to the end of the North Fork Teanaway road, elevation 4243 feet, and hike to Esmerelda Basin (Hike 54). At ¼ mile turn right on the trail signed for Longs Pass and Ingalls Lake. Carry a loaded canteen; the climb can be hot and often is waterless.

The path ascends steadily in fields of grass and blossoms, groves of small trees. Nearby ridges are a startling blend of gray and brown and rusty-red rocks. South beyond Esmerelda Peaks appear Mt. Adams, the Goat Rocks, and Mt. Rainier. At 5600 feet is a junction; the right fork climbs a scant ½ mile to 6250-foot Longs Pass (Hike 56). Go left, swinging around the mountainside into a small valley, winding through buttresses and flowers, joining an older and steeper trail. Just below the pass is a small, green bench with snowmelt (and camps) in early summer. The fi-nal stretch switchbacks to Ingalls Pass, 6500 feet, 3 miles, and a grand view of Mt. Stuart. The way to here is mostly free of snow in late June, while slopes to the north are still white. The ridge can be scrambled in ei-

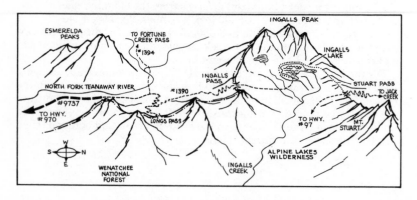

ther direction for higher views.

Contour left on slopes above Headlight Creek Basin, a parkland with cold streams and delightful camps. The way enters a lovely little hanging basin, crosses its creek, descends a bit, then climbs a low ridge of polished brown buttresses—and at last, below is the lake. The way down to the 6463-foot shore is short and easy, but getting around the west (lefthand) side to the outlet requires a ticklish scramble up and down slabs and huge boulders. Don't try the righthand side—it's strictly a rock-climbing route.

From the outlet one can explore to Stuart Pass (Hike 39).

Camping is very limited and firewood nonexistent: anyhow, the lake basin is so heavily pounded it must be a "day-use zone." Camp either in Headlight Creek Basin or below the lake in meadowy headwaters of Ingalls Creek.

Ingalls Lake and Mount Stuart

Mount Stuart from Longs Pass

NORTH FORK TEANAWAY RIVER
Unprotected area

LONGS PASS

Round trip 5 miles
Hiking time 3 hours
High point 6300 feet
Elevation gain 2100 feet
Hikable July through October
One day

Map: Green Trails No. 209 Mount
Stuart
Current information: Ask at Cle
Elum Ranger Station about trail
Nos. 1229 and 1390

Longs Pass is the best seat in the house, front row center, for the big show of 9415-foot Mt. Stuart, without a rival between Rainier and Glacier. Day hikes are the general choice, spending an awed lunchtime gazing across the gulf of Ingalls Creek to the granite cleavers and walls,

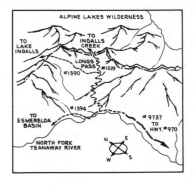

searching with binoculars for goats and climbers. In the idiot times of the not-too-distant past, as soon as the machines were invented, prospectors gouged a cat track to the pass, largely obliterating the old trail. However, a replacement route has been neatly switchbacked and the hike is the most popular in the area.

Drive to the end of North Fork Teanaway road, elevation 4243 feet, and set out on Esmerelda Basin trail No. 1394 (Hike 54). In ¼ mile turn off right on Ingalls Lake–Longs Pass trail No. 1390.

The sparse forest permits views north into Esmerelda Basin and west to Esmerelda Peaks. Trees pretty well give up the struggle to live in the serpentine soils, deficient as they are in certain essential minerals and vitamins, and only plants that can adapt to a poor diet and little water spatter the naked earth with dusty greenery and brilliant blossoms. During the steady, steep ascent the views change abruptly at each switchback as boots and eyes are pointed north to barren red-rock basins, then south to lichen-dark cliffs.

At 2 miles, 5600 feet, the trail splits. Ingalls Lake trail (Hike 55) goes left; go right on trail No. 1229, switchbacking onward and upward over talus, briefly joining the old bulldozer track and, when it heads straight up the slope, resuming a civilized zigzag. At 2½ miles the way crosses a bench with several nice campsites (no water after the snowmelt dries) and quickly attains Longs Pass, 6250 feet.

Climbers commonly camp here to make the ascent of the "dog route" up Stuart, usually in late spring when snow is abundant for cooking into water on stoves. They then descend to Ingalls Creek on remains of an ancient trail or simply plunge down the snow, over talus and through forest. Or they may camp at Ingalls Creek, 4800 feet.

Hikers rarely have any good reason to do that and, if they wish more exercise, scramble the ridge crest north a ways or, in cases of terminal eagerness and a degree of mountaineering skill, traverse the 6878-foot peak and drop to Ingalls Pass (a loop!). Those of milder disposition may follow the bulldozer track south along the ridge 1000 feet and drop to a secluded basin, pleasant camping while the snowmelt lasts.

57 MIDDLE FORK TEANAWAY RIVER

Round trip to Way Creek 7 miles
Hiking time 3 hours
High point 3000 feet
Elevation gain 300 feet
Hikable August through September

One day or backpack
Motorcycle country
Maps: Green Trails No. 209 Mount Stuart and No. 210 Liberty
Current information: Ask at Cle Elum Ranger Station about trail No. 1393

An almost forgotten trail through a picture canyon, by a pleasant stream, to nice campsites, trees, grassy meadows and a surprising amount of solitude caused by five fordings of the stream in the first 3½ miles plus whatever more wading is required by the latest turns taken by the wishy-washy river during the previous winter. The timing of a visit is crucial. The river is much too wild to ford during the snowmelt of early summer. By late summer the wading is easy but the motorcyclists love splashing through the water.

From US 970 drive 7.6 miles on the Teanaway River road, left on the West Fork road 0.7 mile, and then take a right on the Middle Fork road another 4.6 miles to Middle Fork Teanaway River trail No. 1393, elevation 2700 feet.

Here is the first ford. Once across, walk the long-abandoned road, now trail, ¼ mile to the mouth of the canyon. Look down to inviting but inaccessible pools. Within ½ mile the valley widens to forests and interspersed meadows, campsites plentiful. The tread is sometimes wide and smooth, sometimes narrow and rocky, and sometimes—where the trail has been washed away by the wandering river—a bushwhack. At ¾ mile is the second ford, in 1¼ miles the third, in 2 miles the fourth, 3 miles the

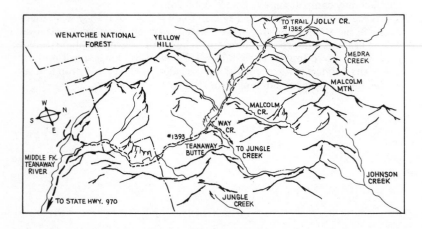

Third crossing of Middle Fork Teanaway River near the headwaters

fifth. At 3½ miles reach the recommended turnabout at the Way Creek–Jungle Creek trail junction (unsigned in 1991), 3000 feet. A few feet farther along is a fine campsite.

The trail continues upvalley, gaining elevation gradually, to more fords, more campsites and more meadows. At 7 miles pass the Jolly Creek trail. From here the way tips upward to the divide above the Salmon la Sac and De Roux country and its network of trails loved by ORVs of all kinds.

58 YELLOW HILL– ELBOW PEAK

Round trip to Elbow Peak 10 miles
Hiking time 5 hours
High point 5673 feet
Elevation gain 2800 feet in, 300 feet out
Hikable mid-June through October

One day
Motorcycle country
Maps: Green Trails No. 208 Kachess Lake and No. 209 Mount Stuart
Current information: Ask at Cle Elum Ranger Station about trail Nos. 1212 and 1222

Even by Teanaway standards the views are outstanding from the sky-open ridge between Yellow Hill and Elbow Peak; the panorama of the Alpine Lakes Wilderness stretches from Mt. Stuart east of the Cascade Crest to Overcoat Peak west of it. The toil up the steep, dry trail is forgotten on the summit, though perhaps not the snarl and whine of the motorcycles ridden here by those who love to feel the wind blow in one ear and out the other.

Drive the Teanaway River road (Hike 45) 7.6 miles from US 970 and go left on West Fork road. In 0.7 mile go right on Middle Fork road No. 113. At 4.6 miles pass the Middle Fork trail. Continue 0.3 mile and turn right on a very rough road to Yellow Hill trail. The hiking mileages given here are from road No. 113, elevation 2800 feet.

Vehicles with various combinations of wheels, tires, and drive trains go one distance or another, but at 1 mile a true trail suddenly appears, heading steeply up the ridge crest while the road makes a switchback, the two rejoining briefly and splitting, the trail to make another lightning ascent while the road switchbacks. At 1½ miles they rejoin again, crest a ridge

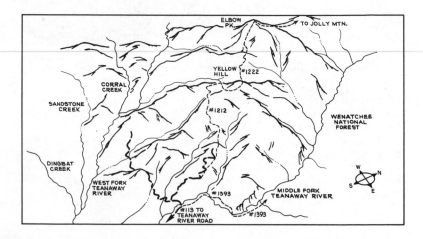

Mount Rainier from Elbow Peak

overlooking the Middle Fork Teanaway valley, and here the road finally gives it up, at 4400 feet.

The trail, now molested only by two-wheelers (and few of them), heads out along the ridge through open pine forest, traversing the west side of Yellow Hill, at 2 miles suddenly veering upward in great contour-leaping strides. While pausing to gasp and shift gears, enjoy the view south over the Middle Fork and West Fork valleys to the main Teanaway River and on out to the Yakima River. Until now the trail number has been 1212, but beyond Yellow Hill it changes to 1222.

At 3 miles Mt. Rainier comes in view, so enormous it seems very near. In ¼ mile more the trail abruptly levels out to contour around Yellow Hill just below the summit, 5500 feet. The way swings to the north slope of the hill, views excellent of Elbow Peak and Jolly Mountain dead ahead and Stuart to the northeast, drops 300 feet to a saddle, and resumes climbing along a thin ridge. In the final ½ mile the path nearly disappears in the rocks, which enclose striking veins of calcite crystals, before the last push up to the grassy summit of Elbow Peak, 5 miles, 5673 feet.

It's far enough for the day. However, the imaginative will note with interest that the trail continues along the ridge 3½ miles to Jolly Mountain (Hike 67), connecting to trails from Salmon la Sac.

59 THORP LAKE

Round trip 6 miles
Allow 3 hours
High point 4750 feet
Elevation gain 1200 feet
Hikable mid-June
through October

One day
Map: Green Trails No. 208 Kachess
Lake
Current information: Ask at Cle
Elum Ranger Station about trail
No. 1316

A rough and sometimes very steep trail to a lake ringed by forest, cliffs, meadows, and campers.

Go off Interstate 90 on Exit 80 and drive the Salmon la Sac road 11 miles beyond the Roslyn (on television known as "Ciceley") City Hall at First and Dakota. Just past the end of Cle Elum Lake (reservoir) turn left on French Cabin Creek road No. 4308 for 3.2 miles and turn right on road No. 4312 another 1.3 miles. On the righthand side find a gated sideroad, the beginning of Thorp Creek trail No. 1316, elevation 3550 feet. (To this point road No. 4312 is maintained; it continues rudely another 1½ miles and if drivable offers a shortcut to Thorp Lake for those with cross-country experience.)

Walk the gated road a short distance, cross Thorp Creek, walk another 200–300 feet to a junction, and turn left about ¼ mile. Just before the road starts climbing go left on an obscure trail. Gaining elevation only modestly, the trail winds across clearcuts and patches of selective logging on both private and Forest Service land. At roughly 1½ miles from the car, the trail tilts upward, at times very steeply, to ascend the rocky headwall.

Several paths branch off left. Stay on the most-used. At 2¾ miles is a junction. The right fork, rather overgrown, proceeds 1½ miles to Thorp Mountain (Hike 61). Go left on the heavily used trail ¼ mile, descending a bit to the shores of Thorp Lake, 4700 feet. Lots of campsites, frequently full to overflowing.

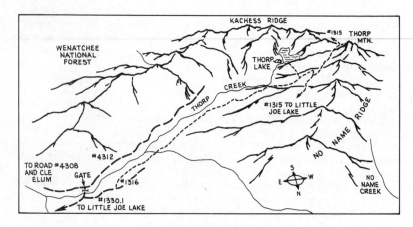

Thorp Lake

Little Joe Lake

CLE ELUM RIVER
Unprotected area

LITTLE JOE–
THORP CREEK LOOP

Loop trip 10 miles
Hiking time 9 hours
High point 5300 feet
Elevation gain 2000 feet
Hikable July through
   October
One day

Maps: Green Trails No. 208 Kachess
   Lake, USGS Polallie Ridge and
   Kachess Lake
Current information: Ask at Cle
   Elum Ranger Station about trail
   Nos. 1315, 1316, and 1330.1

A rough and tough trail, a rugged but rewarding day hike. Though 10 miles don't sound like a lot, finding the way on a frequently obscure trail takes a full day. That's the bad part. The good part is two subalpine lakes, miles of meadowland, views, a historic lookout building, and rather more solitude than can be found elsewhere in the Cle Elum area.

Because the Little Joe Lake trail is easy to lose, the loop is recommended counterclockwise. That strategy also gets the agony of the steepest part over with at the start; the rest will seem a breeze. Though the trail dates from the 1930s or earlier it is not shown on any map.

Drive French Cabin Creek road to the Thorp Creek trailhead (Hike No. 59), elevation 3550 feet.

Walk the gated sideroad across Thorp Creek to a junction. The road to the left is the Thorp Creek trail, the return of the loop. Go straight ahead and in a scant ½ mile from the car cross a creek (for a better name call it Little Joe Creek) and a few feet farther go left on Little Joe Lake trail No. 1330.1.

Take a deep breath because the next 1¼ miles, varying from steep to very steep, gain 1100 feet! That's why this is recommended as a day hike. Maintenance is minimal, so expect blowdowns with a possibility of entirely losing the trail several times. In about 1 mile (on a trail like this who knows?) cross Little Joe Creek. Don't bother searching for the trail, keep within sound of the creek and go straight up to the lake, elevation 4700 feet, 1¾ miles from the car.

Little Joe Lake is too shallow for swimming but has nice campsites. Follow the righthand shore to the inlet stream, on the way crossing a couple of small meadows with little streams. Expect to lose the tread but watch for sawed logs to stay on course. The trail, now better maintained, climbs to a 5000-foot pass, from which it contours 2½ miles through rocky meadows, ascending a bit to join No Name Ridge trail No. 1315 (Hike 63) at 5300 feet. Go left, first on the ridge crest and then along the east slope of Thorp Mountain, 1½ miles to the next junction. Go left (downhill) on Thorp Creek trail No. 1316. If full of beans jaunt on up to the lookout, adding 2 miles round trip and 700 feet of elevation. If short on beans, drop ½ mile down the Thorp Creek trail, steep and sometimes imaginary to the Thorp Lake junction (Hike 59); not many beans are required for the scant ¼ mile sidetrip to the lake. From the lake junction the trail improves for the final 2¾ miles back to the starting point.

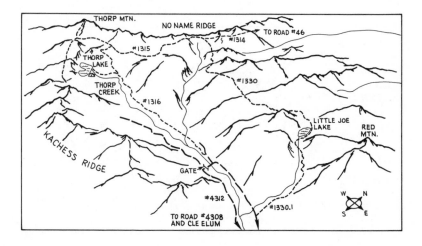

61 THORP MOUNTAIN

Round trip 5 miles
Hiking time 3 hours
High point 5850 feet
Elevation gain 1800 feet
**Hikable late July through mid-
October**

One day
**Map: Green Trails No. 208 Kachess
Lake**
**Current information: Ask at Cle
Elum Ranger Station about trail
Nos. 1315 and 1315A**

Forest ridges and green meadows culminate magnificently in Thorp Mountain Lookout. Views: Rainier, Stuart, Daniel, and the Dutch Miller Gap peaks. Other views, less esthetic: Kachess Lake (reservoir), powerlines, logging roads (which have shrunk the wildland and brought the ridge in easy reach of a day hike).

The views are not the only treasure; late in June the mountain is ablaze with flowers. During the summer of 1945 and 1946 the lookout, Bea Buzzette, a schoolteacher, gathered, identified, and pressed 92 species of plants. Her collection remains on display at the Cle Elum Ranger Station.

The Kachess Ridge trail extends 14¾ miles from road No. 4818, near Easton, to near Cooper Pass (Hike 63). Three good routes reach Thorp Mountain: 4½ miles from French Cabin Creek (Hike 62); a very rough trail up Thorp Creek (Hike 59); or the shortest route, described here, on Knox Creek trail No. 1315A.

Drive the Salmon la Sac road to French Cabin Creek road No. 4308 (Hike 59), turn left on it 5 miles and turn right 2 miles on Knox Creek road No. (4308)120 to the trailhead, elevation 4200 feet.

Knox Creek trail No. 1315A is fairly straightforward, climbing almost entirely in blueberries and flowers. From the road the way switchbacks

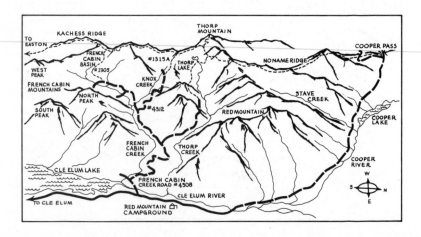

Thorp Mountain Lookout

up a meadow, contours a steep hillside below a cliff, and switchbacks again, enters woods, and at 1¼ miles joins the Kachess Ridge trail No. 1315. Go right on the ridge trail, losing 200 feet, climb another high point, and come out atop a ridge bump 500 feet directly above Thorp Lake. At 1¾ miles is a junction with the Thorp Mountain trail, which switchbacks 400 feet to the lookout at 2½ miles.

The ridge trail proceeds 6½ more miles to road No. (4600)125 near Cooper Pass.

62 FRENCH CABIN MOUNTAIN

Silver Creek Meadows
Round trip 5 miles
Hiking time 3 hours
High point 5000 feet
Elevation gain 900 feet in, 450 feet out
Hikable June through October
One day or backpack
French Cabin Mountain Traverse
One-way trip 8 miles
Hiking time 8 hours

High point 5563 feet
Elevation gain 2600 feet
Hikable mid-June through September
One day
Some illegal motorcycle use on trail No. 1315
Map: Green Trails No. 208 Kachess Lake
Current information: Ask at Cle Elum Ranger Station about trail Nos. 1305, 1308, 1308.1, and 1315

Hike amongst spires of French Cabin Mountain to sprawling fields of grass and flowers at the headwaters of Silver Creek. Delightful campsites are numerous but after the snow melts away only one has water. The meadows can be reached from the town of Easton (Hike 63) or as described here. They make an easy and joyous day hike or, by means of two cars, a very strenuous one-way trip. Much of the way is open to motorcycles but the rangers say very few ever try it.

Drive the Salmon la Sac Road and turn left on French Cabin Creek road No. 4308 (Hike 59).

If using two cars, drive road No. 4308 for 3.8 miles and turn left on road No. (4308)115 for 1.4 miles. Leave one car at Domerie Peak trail No. 1308, located near a big switchback. Drive back to road No. 4308, follow it upvalley 3 miles (6.7 miles from Salmon la Sac road), and turn right 0.7

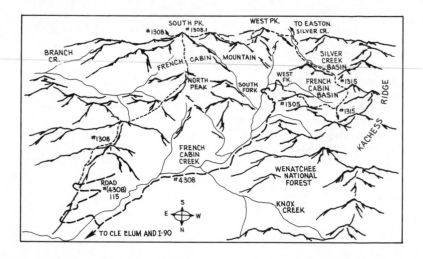

mile on a road signed "French Cabin Creek Trail," elevation 4200 feet. This is trail No. 1305 and the recommended starting point whether ambling only to the meadows or setting out on the traverse.

The trail climbs steadily in trees 1 mile, the views striking of French Cabin Mountain. At 1¼ miles the way enters clearcut private land and comes to a junction. Go left on trail No. 1315, losing 150 feet, then climb between two towering rocks. At about 1¾ miles from the car, reach a 5000-foot pass carpeted with partridgefoot. Views open southward to headwaters of Silver Creek and the destination meadows.

The trail drops steeply a bit to the flat meadowland. The first meadows are grass; farther down the valley the flowers begin. At some 2¾ miles from the car, find obscure (unmarked in 1992) Silver Creek Tie Trail No. 1308.1, going left to a nice campsite with all-summer water, a good turnaround, 4700 feet.

Silver Creek Basin and a spire on French Cabin Mountain

For the one-way trip pass the campsite, cross the creek, and climb, at times on a 20-percent-plus grade, to a 5300-foot shoulder of West Peak and views of Mt. Rainier and ridge-upon-ridge of clearcut-chewed forest.

Next comes a badly eroded trail, dropping 300 feet straight down to a green basin. After that comes a near straight-up climb to a dramatic lunch counter on a nameless 5563-foot high point of French Cabin Mountain. Views are south to Adams and Rainier, east to Ellensburg, and north to glaciered peaks of Dutch Miller Gap.

Again the trail drops, then climbs toward South Peak and a junction with Domerie Peak trail No. 1308. Go left to the 5500-foot summit of South Peak and the last great view. At the top the meadows are a bewilderment of animal trails that are better maintained than the people trail. Keep to the west side of the peak and make certain you are on the trail that goes where people want to go. (We followed an excellent elk trail ¼ mile off on a wrong ridge. However, we were rewarded for the error by the sighting of twelve goats.)

The rest of the way back to the parked car at Domerie Peak trailhead is either steeply up or extremely steeply down, guaranteed to give screaming toes and sore knees.

63 KACHESS RIDGE

One-way trip 14 miles
Hiking time 8 hours
High point 5854 feet
Elevation gain 2600 feet
Hikable July through
  mid-October
One day or backpack

Some illegal motorcycle use
Map: Green Trails No. 208 Kachess
  Lake
Current information: Ask at Cle
  Elum Ranger Station about trail
  No. 1315

An island of wildland isolated by reservoirs west and east, logging roads north, and freeway south is a proper candidate to be placed in a designated wilderness for itself alone. The ridge climaxes in cliffs and flowers of Thorp Mountain. The views are identical (if one can mentally erase reservoirs, clearcuts, and powerlines) to those seen by explorers a century ago—Rainier, Stuart, Daniels, and crags and jags of Dutch Miller Gap. It's best as a one-way trip, requiring the arrangement of transportation at each end. Logic dictates starting at the high end rather than the low, and so the route is here described.

To leave a car at the lower trailhead, drive Interstate 90 east 16.8 miles from Snoqualmie Pass, go off on Lake Easton State Park Exit 70, cross to the north side of the freeway, and turn left on Sparks Road, following "Lake Kachess Dam" signs. In 5 miles take a right on road No. 4818 and in 4 miles another right on the powerline road. At the first junction keep left 1 mile to the trailhead, elevation 2350 feet.

To begin the trip, drive the Salmon la Sac road (Hike 59) 15 miles from Roslyn, to 1 mile short of Salmon la Sac Campground. Turn left on Cooper Lake road No. 46, cross the Cle Elum River, and drive 4.7 miles to Cooper Lake junction. Keep straight ahead on road No. 4600 to Cooper Pass, about 9 miles, and turn left on road No. (4600)125, climbing steeply 3 more miles to trail No. 1315, elevation 4960 feet.

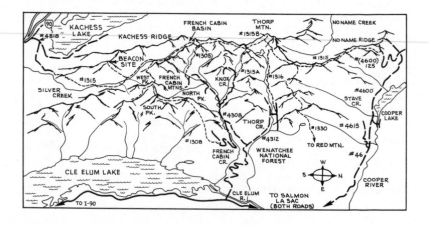

No Name Ridge from Kachess Ridge

The trail works its way up through a clearcut to enter forest, switchbacking up and over a wooded 5083-foot knoll on No Name Ridge, and with few views follows the ridge's ups and downs. At 4 miles cross a 5487-foot hump and pass a junction with Red Mountain trail No. 1330. The way traverses steep slopes on the east side of Thorp Mountain, at 4½ miles passing Thorp Creek trail No. 1316 and at 4¾ miles reaching Thorp Mountain trail No. 1315B. The short sidetrip is mandatory to flowers and views atop Thorp Mountain, 5854 feet (Hike 61).

The ridge trail continues along a narrow crest, climbs steeply, at 5¼ miles passes Knox Creek trail No. 1315A, goes upsy-downsy, descends into a huge clearcut, passes French Cabin Creek trail No. 1305 at 7¼ miles, traverses to a saddle between Kachess Ridge and the west peak of French Cabin Mountain, and enters headwaters of Silver Creek. At 9 miles is trail No. 1308.1, near possible camps. The path continues down, at 14 miles coming to the south trailhead.

Worth noting, in fact worth hiking for its own sake, is the sidetrip to Kachess Beacon Tower, left over from the days when an airway over the Cascades was lighted at night by beacons spotted along the route of the Snoqualmie Pass Highway, the westernmost atop West Tiger Mountain above Issaquah, just east of Seattle. From the south trailhead, hike Silver Creek trail No. 1315 for 2 miles and turn left ¾ mile to the old beacon tower, 4615 feet, for an elevation gain of 2400 feet.

64 SPECTACLE LAKE

Round trip 18½ miles
Allow 2 days
High point 4350 feet
Elevation gain 1550 feet
Hikable August through
September

Map: Green Trails No. 208 Kachess
Lake
Current information: Ask at Cle
Elum Ranger Station about trail
Nos. 1323 and 2000

Only a scattering of miniature glaciers remains of the huge frozen streams that gouged out the Alpine Lakes region of the Cascades. However, the handiwork of ancient ice lies everywhere and is beautifully exhibited by this superb lake in a basin of glacier-polished rock.

Drive Salmon la Sac road (Hike 59) 15 miles from Roslyn and turn left on Cooper Lake road No. 46. Cross the Cle Elum River and proceed 4.7 miles to Cooper Lake junction. Turn right on Cooper Lake road No. 4616 past the recreation area and turn left on road No. (4616)113 a final 1 mile to the trailhead, elevation 2800 feet.

Cooper River trail No. 1323 joins the lakeshore path starting at the campground and follows the Cooper River, rippling beautifully through virgin forest, 5½ miles to Pete Lake, 2980 feet, and much-used and often-crowded campsites. Unravel a confusion of paths at the shelter cabin and find the main trail, which climbs slightly over a rocky rib and drops to a double crossing of two swift creeks at about 7 miles. Both must be crossed. Footlogs may be available; if not, boulder-hopping can be difficult in the high water of early summer. When water is impossibly high, follow Lemah Meadow trail No. 1323B some ¾ mile to the Pacific Crest Trail, which crosses the creeks on bridges; the detour adds 1 mile each way.

Shortly beyond the two creeks, join the Pacific Crest Trail and switchback up toward Chikamin Ridge, mostly in forest, views scarce. At

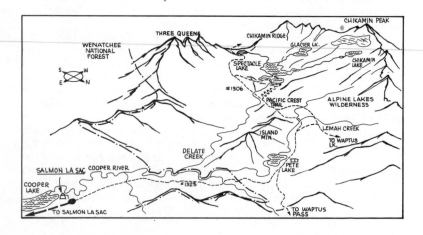

8¾ miles the Crest Trail proceeds onward toward Spectacle Point and Park Lakes and the first of two Spectacle Lake trails branches right.

This first path, called The Staircase because it climbs straight up with trees and roots for footholds, is strenuous but only ½ mile long and compensates by passing a lovely waterfall spilling from the lake, 4350 feet. For the best camps (carry a stove—no fires allowed) cross the outlet just above the falls and walk the south shore. The lake is like an octopus with a half-dozen arms, which makes the shoreline difficult to traverse but provides many glorious camps. To the south rises Three Queens, about 6800 feet. To the northwest is Chikamin Peak and to the north the spectacular spires of 7512-foot Lemah Mountain.

Simply poking about on slabs and buttresses of the lakeshore, admiring polishings and groovings done by the ice and picturesque groupings of trees, can fill out a leisurely visit. But one really ought not miss the smashing views from Spectacle Point. Thread through the confusing maze of upsy-downsy paths south, eventually ending up on the sidetrail that ½ mile from the lake outlet hits the Pacific Crest Trail at ¾ mile from The Staircase start. (If used as the access to the lake, this sidetrail adds 1¼ miles to the approach and a good bit of extra elevation gained and lost, but the walking is easier.) Climb 2 miles to the high-in-the-sky viewpoint, 5475 feet. If ambition continues, proceed on to the next pass (Hike 83).

Spectacle Lake and Lemah Mountain

65

TIRED CREEK–
POLALLIE RIDGE

Round trip to ridge top 11 miles
Hiking time 7 hours
High point 5860 feet
Elevation gain 2600 feet
Hikable late June through
October

One day
Map: Green Trails No. 208 Kachess
Lake
Current information: Ask at Cle
Elum Ranger Station about trail
Nos. 1309, 1317, and 1323

Splendid views are to be had from this high ridge, and though the trail is dry (look to your canteens, troopers) the mouth will water when the eyes drink in Cooper Lake, Dutch Miller Gap's bold rock peaks, and ice-creamy Mt. Hinman and Mt. Daniel, the latter famed as the highest peak in King County.

Pete Lake, Lemah Mountain (left) and Chimney Rock (right) from Polallie Ridge

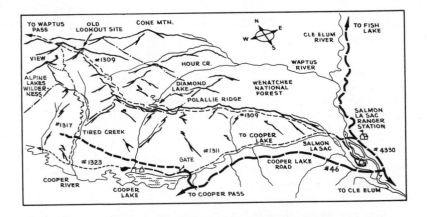

Drive to the Cooper River trailhead, elevation 2800 feet (Hike 64).

Follow Pete Lake trail No. 1323 along the Cooper River 1 flat mile and turn right and up on Tired Creek trail No. 1317. In a long ¼ mile cross an abandoned logging road and be guided by signs on a bulldozed fire trail that climbs steeply around a clearcut and at the top joins the old trail, a rough but adequate path ascending steadily with many switchbacks. Views begin at the road and get better as elevation is gained. At about 1¾ miles two switchbacks on the edge of a ridge offer a look west to Pete Lake. At 2 miles forest yields to meadowlands as the trail traverses under the ridge and aims for a wooded pass at the head of Tired Creek.

The best views are from the top of this ridge, a logical turnaround for day-hikers and an absolutely mandatory sidetrip for those continuing on. Leave the trail at any convenient spot, scramble to the crest, and walk to the highest point, 5360 feet, a great place to soak up scenery and spend the day watching shadows move across distant mountains.

Many goodies remain in store for hikers choosing to continue. Descend from the view crest to regain the trail and contour to the wooded pass, 5280 feet, 3 miles from the abandoned logging road, and a bit beyond to a junction. The left fork drops 2 miles to Waptus Pass; for a 15-mile loop trip, return to the car via this pass and Pete Lake (Hike 64).

The right fork climbs a scant ¼ mile to the site of the old Polallie Ridge lookout, 5482 feet. Amid fragrant meadows settle down to swig the jug of raspberry punch and eat a Cadbury with cashews while gazing all around to magnificent mountains and deep, green valleys.

For a different loop, continue on Polallie Ridge trail 5½ miles downhill, then the Cooper River trail 3½ miles upstream (Hikes 68 and 71), returning to the campground at Cooper Lake and thence to your car for a total loop of 16 miles.

66 MINERAL CREEK PARK

**Round trip from Cooper Pass
road 10 miles
Hiking time 8 hours
High point 4700 feet
Elevation gain 2300 feet
Hikable July through
October
One day or backpack
Round trip from Kachess Lake
Campground 20 miles**

**Allow 2 days
High point 4700 feet
Elevation gain 3300 feet
Hikable July through October
Maps: Green Trails No. 207
Snoqualmie Pass and
No. 208 Kachess Lake
Current information: Ask at Cle
Elum Ranger Station about trail
No. 1331**

Lakes and ponds and marshes amid heather and huckleberry, views from meadows, views from ridges. The trail is steep and rocky and brushy, a slow-going ankle-twister and leg-breaker, but so short it is thronged on weekends.

Once upon a time—until 1968, in fact—the trip began with a lovely lakeside trail along Kachess Lake. Now, in the name of progress, a logging road has intersected the route right in the middle, cutting the hike in half. Since the challenge and satisfaction of traveling the entire distance in unmarred wilderness have been lost, the most practical plan probably is to use the new road as an approach to the upper half and maybe some other day walk the lower half.

To reach the halfway point, drive to Cooper Lake junction (Hike 64) and keep straight on road No. 46, climbing 2.1 miles to Cooper Pass and dropping 2.5 miles into the Kachess valley, to Mineral Creek trail No. 1331, signed "Park Lake 6," elevation 2400 feet. The "Hiker Only" trail crosses the valley-bottom clearcut and river gravels, fords Mineral Creek, and climbs to join the old mining road-become-trail from Kachess Lake.

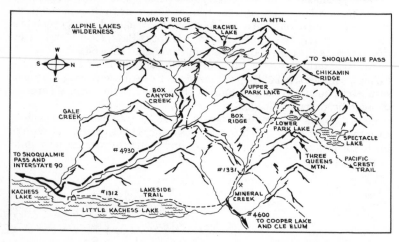

Laside Trail No. 1312 follows the lake more than 3 miles to its head, never over 200–400 feet above the water, but seldom level and with so many ups and downs that about 1000 feet of elevation are gained and lost. At the end of the lake the footpath merges into a mining road built in the days of the Model T and now abandoned. At about 4¹/₂ miles the route turns up Mineral Creek trail No. 1331, climbing steeply; here is the junction with the access from the logging road, the beginning of the short version of the trip.

The "mining" road continues 1¹/₄ miles to an end at ruins of the prospectors' camp. From here the tread just grew, going up and down and around, never level, often very steep. Most of the way is brushed out regularly—thankfully, because much of it is in slick alder and vine maple. Beyond the mine ¹/₄ mile the trail crosses Mineral Creek and enters the Alpine Lakes Wilderness; until safely in those protected forests be prepared for continuing vile deeds by Plum Creek, heir of the Northern Pacific land grab. Tolerable camps are at the mine, the crossing of the outlet stream of Lower Park Lake, 3³/₄ miles, and halfway between. At the end of a straight-up stretch the path abruptly flattens into meadow country and passes near Upper Park Lake, 4700 feet, 5 miles. Camp only at designated sites and build no fires; please cooperate with the backcountry rangers in the meadow restoration project they have in progress. Other and pleasanter and lonesomer camps are strewn about the headwaters basin of Mineral Creek; for the best, avoid the lakes.

For the memorable trip continue ¹/₄ mile to join the Pacific Crest Trail at 4970 feet, then climb left to the pass overlooking Gold Creek or right to Spectacle Point jutting into the sky above Spectacle Lake (Hike 64).

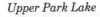
Upper Park Lake

67 JOLLY MOUNTAIN

Round trip from Salmon la Sac
12 miles
Hiking time 7–8 hours
High point 6443 feet
Elevation gain 4003 feet
Hikable July through
September

One day
Motorcycle country
Map: Green Trails No. 208 Kachess
Lake
Current information: Ask at Cle
Elum Ranger Station about trail
Nos. 1307 and 1340

An eastern outpost of the Alpine Lakes Cascades gives 360-degree views east to Mt. Stuart and the freeway leading into Ellensburg, north to Mt. Daniel, west to Pete Lake and the Dutch Miller Gap peaks, south to Mt. Rainier, and directly down to Cle Elum Lake.

Drive Salmon la Sac road (Hike 59) 15.5 miles from Roslyn to just short of the Salmon la Sac Campground and a historic old log building. Turn right on the Cayuse (that's a horse) Campground road to the trailhead parking area near a Forest Service horse barn, elevation 2400 feet.

Go left of the barn to find the trailhead at the edge of the public corral. In ¼ mile briefly touch a service road and then return to trail, which climbs steeply with many switchbacks to a difficult crossing (easier by late July) of Salmon la Sac Creek. This is the only certain water on the entire route. At 2 miles cross a Plum Creek Company clearcut. At 3½ miles is a junction with the Paris Creek trail; keep right. The way ascends the valley a bit farther and then starts a series of switchbacks up the hill-

side. At 4½ miles is a junction with the Sasse Mountain sheep drive-way (to use this as an alternate approach, see below). Pass trail No. 1353 and in ¼ mile stay right at a junction with the Jolly Creek trail. Go right, climbing steeply amid growing views the final 1¼ miles to the 6443-foot summit, site of a fire lookout removed in 1968.

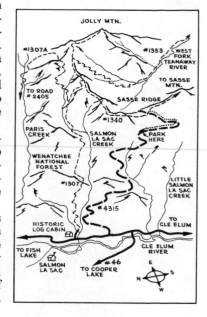

A jolly place to sop up panoramas. Carry a state road map to identify landmarks far out in Eastern Washington and a Forest Service map to name the innumerable peaks.

Though there may be snowfields to traverse then and the creek is difficult to cross, a magnificent time for the trip is June, when the way lies through fields of glacier lilies, spreading phlox, and lanceleaf spring beauty. Unfortunately, a

Mount Stuart from Jolly Mountain

band of sheep occasionally summers in the area and some of the meadows may be close-cropped and stinky.

An alternate approach saves about 3000 feet of climbing. Just 0.6 mile south of the Cayuse Campground find Little Salmon la Sac road No. 4315 (closed in some seasons) and drive 6.5 miles to an elevation of about 5400 feet, where the road intersects the Sasse Mountain sheep driveway on the crest of Sasse Ridge. Be warned. The last 2 miles are steep, narrow, and mighty scary. This is part of the Plum Creek Company road system and may not be maintained. Follow the sheep trail north a little over a mile to the junction with the Salmon la Sac trail and proceed to the top of Jolly Mountain.

If transportation can be arranged, a good loop trip can be made by going up the Little Salmon la Sac road and down the Jolly Mountain trail.

68 COOPER RIVER

One-way trip to Cooper Lake 4
  miles
Hiking time 2 hours
High point 2800 feet
Elevation gain 400 feet
Hikable June through
  October

One day or backpack
Map: Green Trails No. 208 Kachess
  Lake
Current information: Ask at Cle
  Elum Ranger Station about trail
  No. 1311

Solitude and untrammeled wilderness—this is not the hike for that. The forest path along rocky banks of the swift-flowing Cooper River is thronged with enthusiastic Scouts, families, large groups of friends, two-somes, and singles enjoying sauntering walks or picnics, watching the birds, watching the water, studying flowers and trees, and generally having a good time. Part of the fun of this trip is seeing how much fun people have on a trail. Wear a happy face and make friends.

Drive Salmon la Sac road (Hike 59) to Salmon la Sac and cross the Cle Elum River bridge. Just beyond, at the campground entrance, turn right and drive 0.5 mile to the Waptus River trail (Hike 69)/Cooper River trailhead, elevation 2400 feet.

The combined trails follow Cooper River upstream a short ¼ mile. At the first Y go left on Cooper River trail No. 1311. Viewpoints of the river beckon. Green pools invite. At ½ mile, 2480 feet, Polallie Ridge trail No. 1309 (Hikes 65 and 71) branches right; it, too, may be disrupted by logging to come.

In the next mile the path gains 300 feet, then remains nearly level to the lake, weaving through trees. At 2½ miles the way diverges from the river to cross a small creek from Polallie Ridge and returns to the river. From the far side come occasional sounds of vehicles on the Cooper River road. At 4 miles the trail crosses road No. 4616 and drops into Owhi Campground on the shores of Cooper Lake, 2788 feet, a good turnaround for day-hikers; whether a backpacker would care to bed down here among the car-campers is questionable.

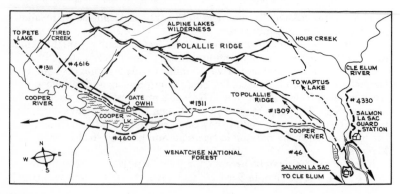

A common way to exploit the trail as a one-way trip is for part of a family or group to drive to the lake for a picnic, the rest to walk there. All or some of this group (or any other) may be pleased to take the 3-mile around-the-lake trail, with a degree of solitude and nice views over the water to forested ridges.

Cooper Lake

69   WAPTUS RIVER

**Round trip to Waptus Lake 16
  miles**
Allow 2 days
High point 2963 feet
**Elevation gain about 1000 feet,
  including ups and downs**

**Hikable July through
  October**
**Maps: Green Trails No. 176 Stevens
  Pass and No. 208 Kachess Lake**
**Current information: Ask at Cle
  Elum Ranger Station about trail
  Nos. 1310 and 2000**

The largest lake in the Alpine Lakes region, 2 miles long and ³/₈ mile
wide, dominates a glacier-gouged trough that also is one of the area's hug-
est. In a calm sunrise the still waters so mirror the snows of Summit
Chief Mountain and the spectacular spire of 7197-foot Bears Breast
Mountain as to guarantee an epiphany. Don't sleep in. Nor go to bed too
early—the Bears Breast silhouette backlighted by sunset is enough to
drop a mountain climber to his knees in fear and trembling.

Drive to Salmon la Sac (Hike 68) and cross the Cle Elum River bridge.
Just beyond, at the edge of the campground, go right 0.7 mile to Waptus
River trail No. 1310, elevation 2400 feet.

The trail begins with a gradual ascent along the Cooper River. In a
short ¼ mile, at a Y, stay right and enter the Alpine Lakes Wilderness. At
1½ miles, 2900 feet, top the low divide and drop to the Waptus valley floor
at the easy ford of Hour Creek, about 2½ miles. The camp here is rather
horsey; hikers will be happier in any of the numerous small riverside sites
farther up the valley.

The trail now climbs 300 feet, again drops a little, and at about 4 miles
touches the bank of the Waptus River. Views here of 5295-foot Cone
Mountain rise above the route ahead. The way henceforth remains close
to the river, whose clear waters sometimes dance over boulders, other
times flow so quietly and smoothly they seem not to move at all.

At about 5½ miles the trail rounds the base of Cone Mountain, opening
views toward the head of the valley, and at 8 miles reaches a junction.
The left fork leads along the west shore of Waptus Lake and climbs

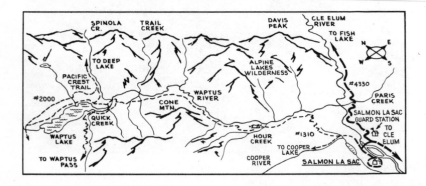

Summit Chief (left) and Bears Breast (right) from Waptus Lake

Polallie Ridge (Hike 71) to Waptus Pass and Pete Lake (Hike 64).

The Waptus trail goes right, turning downvalley ¼ mile to a steel-and-wood bridge over the river, then heading upvalley again to cross Spinola Creek and join Spinola Creek trail No. 1310A coming from Deep Lake (Hike 75). At 8½ miles the path arrives at Waptus Lake, 2963 feet, and a wonderful campsite with great views of mountains in the sky and their reflections in the water. However, this is also the most crowded camp; for other lakeside sites follow the trail 1½ miles along the shore.

The trail continues up the Waptus valley, ascending moderately 3½ miles; along the way, at Spade Creek, it joins the Pacific Crest Trail and the two proceed as one to the Upper Waptus River bridge. Here the gentle climbing ends. As the Crest Trail goes off left to switchback up Escondido Ridge, Dutch Miller Gap trail No. 1362 goes right, switchbacking 1400 feet in 2½ miles to Lake Ivanhoe at 4652 feet, 15 miles from the road. At 16 miles the trail reaches the 5000-foot summit of Dutch Miller Gap (Hike 96).

Air view of Spade and Venus Lakes below Mount Daniel; for a close-up view of the polished rocks at Spade Lake, see page 25.

CLE ELUM RIVER
Alpine Lakes Wilderness

70   SPADE LAKE

**Round trip from the road
  28 miles
Allow 3 days
High point 5400 feet
Elevation gain 3400 feet
Hikable mid-July through
  September
Round trip from Waptus Lake 8
  miles
Hiking time 6 hours**

**High point 5400 feet
Elevation gain 2400 feet
Hikable mid-July through
  September
Maps: Green Trails No. 176 Stevens
  Pass and No. 208 Kachess Lake
Current information: Ask at Cle
  Elum Ranger Station about trail
  No. 1357**

A high and very beautiful alpine lake under the tall southern buttresses of Mt. Daniel. The deep blue waters, generally frozen until the middle of July, are surrounded by bare, rounded rock whose striations tell the story of the glacier that carved this cirque not so many thousand years ago.

The Spade Lake trail, originally a sheep driveway, is extremely steep and badly eroded and lies on a south-facing slope, which though largely

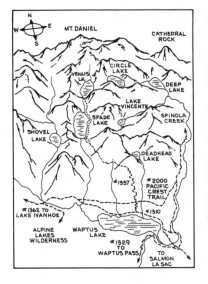

White heather

shaded can be hot and dry; on sunny days set out from Waptus Lake no later than 7 A.M. The approximately 4-mile route takes from 3 to 5 hours up and 2 to 3 hours down—and to get to the beginning one must first hike 9½ miles up the Waptus River.

Drive to Salmon la Sac and hike to Waptus Lake (Hike 69). Follow the trail around the north shore a scant mile and at 9½ miles from the road find Spade Lake trail No. 1337, elevation 3000 feet.

The "Hiker Only" trail is rough and steep as it climbs rapidly, crossing the Pacific Crest Trail, and becomes rougher and steeper as it shoots straight up the hillside, gaining 1200 feet in about 1½ miles to 4200 feet. The climb then eases, alternating between steep ascents and maddening short descents. The path remains difficult as the views grow, including an aerial perspective on Waptus Lake. The first reliable water is at 2½ miles, 5200 feet. At 3 miles, 5400 feet, is a dramatic view of the summit spire of Bears Breast rising above huge, slabby cliffs and of glaciers on 7300-foot Summit Chief. The Dutch Miller Gap trail can be seen switch-backing up the opposite hillside. About now one can look ahead to glacier-polished rock at the outlet of Spade Lake and to the southern cliffs of Mt. Hinman, a small piece of glacier showing. A last rugged mile of many little ups and downs leads to the lake at 5210 feet.

Campsites are located near the outlet, on a peninsula halfway around the south shore, and in heather meadows above the lake. The meadows are ribbed by outcrops of polished rock, making travel slow. Don't camp on the heather—once broken down it takes years to regrow.

A worthwhile sidetrip is Venus Lake, 5672 feet. Follow a fishermen's path ¾ mile along the east side of Spade Lake and climb the rocks just to the right of the waterfall another ¾ mile. Except for the narrow outlet (room for several campers) Venus Lake is walled in by naked cliffs.

171

71 WAPTUS PASS LOOP

Basic loop 21 miles
Allow 2–4 days
High point 5547 feet
Elevation gain 3147 feet
Hikable mid-July through mid-September

Map: Green Trails No. 208 Kachess Lake
Current information: Ask at Cle Elum Ranger Station about trail Nos. 1309, 1310, and 1329

Here's a loop to pump up a connoisseur of looping. Link the Waptus River trail to the Cooper River trail via the green meadows of Waptus Pass and the wide-view heights of Polallie Ridge. Add a couple of extra days to extend the loop to one or more subalpine lakes and another high vista from a rib of Summit Chief Mountain. Be forewarned—this is horse country and by the end of summer the trail is mighty rough and dusty and stinky.

Drive to Salmon la Sac (Hike 68) and the start of Waptus River trail No. 1310 (Hike 69), elevation 2400 feet.

Hike along the Waptus River, passing excellent camps at 2½ and 6 miles. At 8 miles the horse and foot trails to 2963-foot Waptus Lake diverge. Good camps lie ¾ mile along both. Those on the footpath have splendid views of Bears Breast and Summit Chief Mountains but usually are very busy. Those on the horse-ford path are more secluded but less scenic and sanitary.

The loop route follows the horse trail ½ mile to a split where the beasts turn right to ford the river; go left ¼ mile to another fork. The right fork leads ¼ mile to lakeshore camps; go left and steeply ascend the forested gorge of Quick Creek. At 2 miles from the lake the angle eases and at 3 miles are marshy meadows of Waptus Pass, 4320 feet. Here is a trail junction, the right to Escondido Lake and the Waptus Burn trail and the left, the loop route, to Polallie Ridge. The pass has two nice camps, one just before the junction and one just beyond.

The Polallie Ridge trail, boggy in spots and with some windfall, ascends

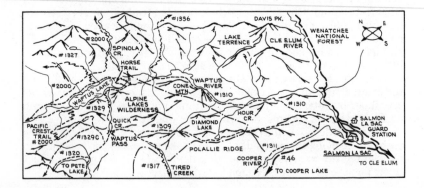

Waptus Pass

the crest, in woods and opens, with few views and lots of horse droppings, 1½ miles to Tired Creek trail (Hike 65) from the Cooper River, and ¼ mile more to the site of Polallie Ridge Lookout, 5482 feet. This is the climax vista of the loop, so get out the squirrel food and banana chips and count the major summits: Cathedral Rock, Daniel, Hinman, Bears Breast, Summit Chief, Overcoat, Chimney Rock, Lemah, Chikamin, Three Queens, and, of course, Rainier.

Beyond the lookout site ½ mile the trail passes the highest, but forested, point of the ridge, 5547 feet, and shortly splits. The left fork is the official trail. Keep right on the crest another ¼ mile to milk the last panoramas, then drop to a marshy bench on the east slope of the ridge, reclimb to the crest, and repeat the procedure. The third descent reaches Diamond Lake, 5060 feet, 4½ miles from Waptus Pass, and several well-defined camps.

The way climbs over one final rib and begins the long run down the lowering crest of Polallie Ridge to the foot, where Cooper River trail (Hike 68) leads ½ mile back to Salmon la Sac.

Variations on the basic loop: from Waptus Lake hike the Pacific Crest Trail 6½ miles to a 5700-foot shoulder of Summit Chief, then Waptus Burn trail No. 1329C for 2½ miles to Waptus Pass. Or, stay on the Crest Trail a mile beyond this junction, take the bootpath down to Escondido Lake, follow the rather marshy trail to the Pete Lake trail, and return to the basic loop at Waptus Pass. Or if too dizzy to stop looping, let your imagination run wild all the way to Pete Lake and wherever.

72 DAVIS PEAK

Round trip 11 miles
Hiking time 8 hours
High point 6426 feet
Elevation gain 3900 feet
Hikable (in part) May through October

One day
Map: Green Trails No. 208 Kachess Lake
Current information: Ask at Cle Elum Ranger Station about trail No. 1324

A long, hot, dry hike in open forest, repaid by views of the Snoqualmie Pass peaks, Mt. Daniel, and forests of the Waptus valley from a lookout peak overlooking the Salmon la Sac region. The eastern slopes of the Cascades often have sunshine while the westside peaks are lost in clouds, so start in early morning.

Drive to Salmon la Sac (Hike 68). Just before crossing the river go right on road No. 4330 for 1.7 miles, turn left on road No. (4330)134 past private residences, and in 0.4 mile go left; in a final rough 0.2 mile reach Mt. Davis trail No. 1324, elevation 2550 feet.

In ¼ mile the trail crosses the Cle Elum River on a bridge, goes about ¼ mile, then comes out on a logging road on private property. Follow the road straight ahead, watching closely for the trail on the left. After leaving the logging road, the way is through forest a full mile, in the course of which it reenters national forest and commences relentless switchbacks due north up the mountainside. Around the 2-mile mark the trees thin, allowing views east and south. The trail zigzags, traverses the valley head, and then zigzags up to the old lookout site.

Views are unlimited over the Salmon la Sac area, the Wenatchee Mountains, the Cle Elum valley, and mountains, mountains, mountains. The crest of Davis Peak is shaped like the shoe of a westward-running horse, the lookout on one of the heel tips and Opal Lake on the other. A trail goes west along the edge of the cliffs to the true summit, West Point, at the "toe" of the horseshoe, from which the view is across Waptus Lake to Dutch Miller Gap, 10 crow-miles away.

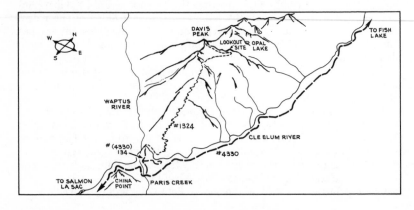

Davis Peak trail

Jack Creek valley from Scatter Creek Pass

CLE ELUM RIVER
Unprotected area

73 SCATTER CREEK PASS–PADDY-GO-EASY PASS LOOP

Round trip to Fish Eagle Pass 9 miles
Hiking time 6 hours
High point 6200 feet
Elevation gain 2880 feet
Hikable mid-July through September
One day
Loop trip 23 miles
Allow 2–3 days

High point 6200 feet
Elevation gain 4800 feet
Hikable mid-July through September
Maps: Green Trails No. 176 Stevens Pass and No. 177 Chiwaukum Mountains
Current information: Ask at Cle Elum Ranger Station about trail Nos. 1328 and 1595

A lonesome meadow high on the Wenatchee Mountains reached by a one-time (and sometimes still) sheep driveway. A great day hike. The route also lends itself to a long but rewarding loop trip over two passes and miles of seldom-traveled streamside trail.

Due to routefinding problems (including the fact that the usually accurate USGS and Forest Service maps show the trail where it isn't) it's best to start on the Scatter Creek end.

Drive to Salmon la Sac (Hike 68) and continue 9 miles on road No. 4330 to Scatter Creek crossing (the creek is underground most of the summer). Find Scatter Creek trail No. 1328, signed "County Line Trail 2 miles," elevation 3320 feet.

Obscure at the start, the trail soon becomes evident as it ascends virtually straight up, no switchbacks, 1500 feet to a junction. County Line Trail No. 1394.1 goes right. Go left over Scatter Creek, the trail again evasive and easily lost in sheep-trampled meadows. Several campsites are passed (delightful if the sheep haven't been there lately) as the path generally follows the creek upward to Fish Eagle Pass at 6200 feet, 4½ miles. (Some maps call it "Scatter Creek Pass" but the Forest Service says that's someplace else.) If returning this way, make careful note of where the creek was crossed; miss that spot and you may be in trouble. The pass makes an excellent turnaround for a day hike.

For the loop, take the obvious trail switchbacking down Solomon Creek to Jack Creek trail No. 1558 at 8 miles, 4000 feet. Go downstream through forest 2½ miles to a junction, 10½ miles, 3800 feet. Turn left on Meadow Creek trail No. 1559, which climbs gently (mostly) 4½ miles to a wooded pass at 5400 feet and drops 1 mile in French Creek drainage to the junction, 16 miles, 4750 feet, with Paddy-Go-Easy Pass–French Creek trail No. 1595. Go left, zigzagging up 1400 feet in 2 miles to Paddy-Go-Easy Pass, 6950 feet (Hike 74). Here you may encounter the first other hikers of the trip. Views are fine out to Mt. Daniel. Flowers bloom in mid-July, even though Sprite Lake, nestled in a small cirque, may be frozen until August. No firewood remains at the lake. Thanks (no thanks) to the archaic 1872 Mining Laws, both the pass and the lake are private land, a good reason to abolish the rotten old law.

From the pass drop 2700 feet in 3 miles to the Cle Elum River road and walk 2 miles on the road past Tucquala (Fish) Lake to Scatter Creek.

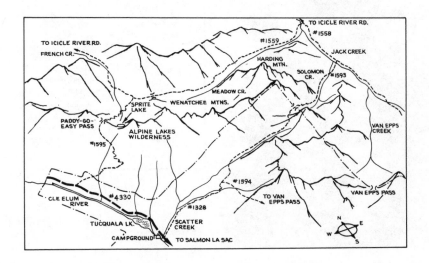

74 PADDY-GO-EASY PASS

Round trip to pass 6 miles
Hiking time 4 hours
High point 6100 feet
Elevation gain 2700 feet
Hikable mid-July through
September

One day or backpack
Map: Green Trails No. 176 Stevens
Pass
Current information: Ask at Cle
Elum Ranger Station about trail
No. 1595

A short, steep climb to a high pass with views out to great peaks and down to Fish Lake (Tucquala Lake) and the marshy valley of the Cle Elum River, and then an easy meadow-roaming walk to a lovely little lake. Flowers bloom here in mid-July but the lake is generally frozen until the end of the month.

Drive to Salmon la Sac (Hike 68) and continue 11.4 miles on road No. 4330, to about 0.7 mile past Fish Lake Guard Station, and find the trailhead, elevation 3400 feet, on the right side of the road behind a group of tumbledown private cabins along a stream.

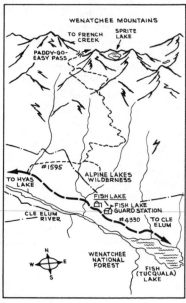

Sprite Lake

Paddy-Go-Easy Pass trail No. 1595 starts in woods and in ½ mile passes a creek, the last water for 2 miles. At 1 mile is a junction with an abandoned trail going to the guard station; keep left. The way now steepens, switchbacking up through dense timber to small meadows with views to the valley and to Cathedral Rock and Mt. Daniel. At about 2½ miles the trail forks (unmarked). The left fork switchbacks directly to the pass. The right fork detours by an old mine and a stream, rejoining the main trail ¼ mile below the pass. The final stretch traverses under red cliffs of a 6500-foot peak to Paddy-Go-Easy Pass, 3½ miles, 6100 feet.

The east slopes of the pass are mostly meadowland. Contour south along the ridge ¼ mile to a point directly above 6000-foot Sprite Lake and descend to the shores. Delightful campsites, no fires allowed, so carry a stove. The tiny lake provides a striking foreground for The Cradle, the impressive 7467-foot peak across the valley.

75 CATHEDRAL ROCK– DECEPTION PASS LOOP

Loop trip 14 miles
Allow 2–4 days
High point 5500 feet
Elevation gain 2300 feet
Hikable July through
September

Map: Green Trails No. 176 Stevens
Pass
Current information: Ask at Cle
Elum Ranger Station about trail
Nos. 1345, 1376, and 2000

The basic ramble around the head of the old Cle Elum Glacier trough, in meadows and by waterfalls and tarns, amid spectacularities of the Alpine Lakes Wilderness, can be done in a couple of easy days. However, two or three more should be allowed for sidetrips to some of the region's most eye-bugging scenery.

Drive to Salmon la Sac (Hike 68) and continue 12.5 miles on road No. 4330 to the end at the Hyas Lake–Deception Pass trailhead, elevation 3350 feet.

From the parking area walk the road back a short bit to the last Y, go west a similar distance to the start of Cathedral Rock trail No. 1345, and follow it to Cathedral Pass, 4¹/₂ miles, 5500 feet (Hike 77). On the way, at 2¹/₂ miles, 4841 feet, is Squaw Lake, the last good camp that has year-round water. From the intersection at Cathedral Pass the Pacific Crest Trail drops left to Deep Lake (Hike 76), the first of the possible sidetrips. To the right it heads for Deception Pass. Also from the intersection starts the second possible sidetrip, on a very rude and rather risky semi-path to Peggy's Pond.

The next 4¹/₂ miles of the Crest Trail between Cathedral and Deception passes is scenery all the way, views extending from the alpine gardens over the ground-down-at-the-heel glacial trough and its characteristic marshy lakes, Hyas and Fish, up to the long and blocky ridge of Granite Mountain. At places the Crest Freeway was dynamited, at enormous ex-

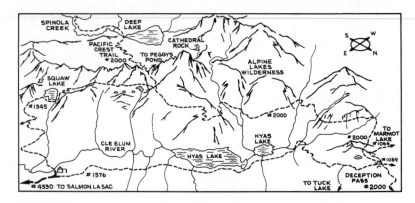

Cathedral Rock

pense, in cliffs plunging from the summit of Cathedral Rock and spur ridges of Mt. Daniel. (Note: The trail has two stream crossings that in the high water of snowmelt season or cloudbursts are formidable to the point of suicidal. Many a party has been forced to turn back and make a long detour via the Cle Elum valley floor; when in doubt, call the Forest Service before setting out.)

At 9 miles from the road the loop reaches Deception Pass, 4475 feet, and intersects the Marmot Lake trail, the third good sidetrip (Hike 78). Camps near the pass lack water after the snowmelt dries up, but a year-round dribble can be found ½ mile down the Hyas Lake trail, near the takeoff of the Tuck and Robin Lakes trail, the fourth sidetrip (Hike 77).

The loop is completed with a quick descent to the floor of the trough and a passage along the shore of Hyas Lake to the road-end, finishing off the last of the 14 miles.

76

DEEP LAKE

Round trip 14½ miles
Hiking time 9 hours
High point 5500 feet
Elevation gain 2150 feet in, 1200 feet out
Hikable July through October

One day or backpack
Map: Green Trails No. 176 Stevens Pass
Current information: Ask at Cle Elum Ranger Station about trail Nos. 1345 and 2000

Climb in forest to beautiful meadow country at the base of Cathedral Rock. Look in one direction down to the Cle Elum River and beyond to Mt. Stuart, highest summit in the Alpine Lakes Wilderness, and in the other to 7960-foot Mt. Daniel, highest summit in King County. Look below to

Shoulder of Mount Daniel and outlet of Deep Lake

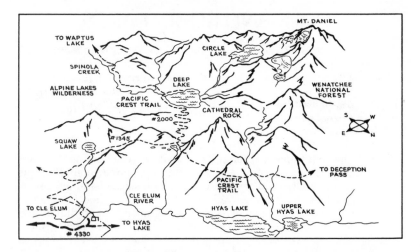

the green valley of Spinola Creek and, at its head, under the slopes of
Daniel, the blue waters of Deep Lake.

Drive to Salmon la Sac (Hike 68) and continue 12.5 miles on road No.
4330 to a Y a short bit from the road-end. The right spur goes a few dozen
yards to the Hyas Lake–Deception Pass trailhead. Take the left spur a
similar distance to the Deep Lake trailhead, elevation 3350 feet.

Cathedral Rock trail No. 1345 crosses the Cle Elum River on a bridge
and ascends steadily but moderately in cool forest, at 2 miles passing a
junction with Trail Creek trail No. 1322. At 2½ miles the trail emerges
into marshy meadows around the shores of little Squaw Lake, 4841 feet, a
pleasant picnic spot and a good turnaround for an easy afternoon.

The way continues up in subalpine forest and patches of flowers and
growing views, traverses heather gardens along the ridge slopes, and at
4½ miles, 5500 feet, reaches Cathedral Pass, nearly at the foot of Cathedral Rock, at this point intersecting the Pacific Crest Trail coming from
Deception Pass.

To descend or not to descend—that is the question. The views from the
saddle make it a satisfying destination, and parkland on the ridge crest
invites wandering; in early summer, snowmelt ponds permit delightful
camps.

If the lake is chosen, descend 1200 feet on the Crest Trail, which drops
to forest in a long series of switchbacks, at 7¼ miles from your trailhead
arriving on the east side of Deep Lake, 4382 feet. Camp at sites in the adjoining forest but *not* on the shores.

The Crest Trail proceeds down Spinola Creek to the Waptus River.

77 TUCK AND ROBIN LAKES

Round trip to Robin Lakes 14 miles
Allow 3–4 days
High point 6250 feet
Elevation gain 3200 feet
Hikable August through mid-October

Map: Green Trails No. 176 Stevens Pass
Current information: Ask at Cle Elum Ranger Station about trail Nos. 1376 and 1376A

Since the requirement of permits to visit the Enchantment Lakes, Robin Lakes have what often seems the largest alpine population this side of the winter Olympics. The Forest Service tried to discourage use by canceling plans to build a real trail. We cooperated by removing the trip from a previous edition of this book. But in our age of wildland (and world) overpopulation there's no keeping a secret. The new management goal is not to hide the place but keep it from being pounded and burned and polluted to death. A permit system surely must come soon.

Drive from Salmon la Sac to the Hyas Lake–Deception Pass trailhead, elevation 3350 feet (Hike 75).

Walk the valley trail to Hyas Lake at 1½ miles, 3448 feet. The mile-long lake, ringed by forest and reedy marsh, watched over by the tower of 6724-foot Cathedral Rock, has many pleasant camps and is popular among novices trying out new gear and families trying out new kids. Beyond the lake, at a scant 4 miles, the trail turns steeply up, switch-backing. At some 4½ miles, 4300 feet, while still a long ½ mile from Deception Pass, the way gentles. Watch for a trail sign.

An ancient firemen's track, unbuilt, unmaintained, dips to cross two small creeks, bumps against the forest wall, and begins an ingenious alternation of contours to get above or under cliffs and straight-up scrambles to get through them.

A short bit past a rock promontory in an old burn (stunning views) at 6

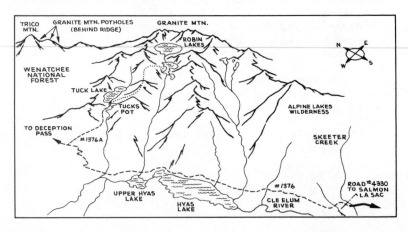

Mount Daniel from Robin Lake

miles, 5268 feet, the path levels out to Tuck Lake, surrounded by cliffs. Every square foot of flat ground is either an "established camp" or an "established toilet"—and is in the middle of a path to somewhere—and on a fine weekend is occupied. Except for the small area in the woods where the trail first touches the lake, firewood is zero, and that's good because fires are not permitted. For peaceful and neat camping you'll do better in a zoo.

From the lake outlet take any of the paths along the divider ridge and when it leaps upward ascend to the crest at 5800 feet. Cairns and tread lead along the crest, down and up the side of the ridge to its merger into the mountainside at 6000 feet, then up heather and slabs to a 6250-foot shoulder, and at 1 mile from Tuck, down to Lower Robin Lake, 6163 feet, which connects to Upper Robin, 6178 feet.

Roam as you please in the wide-open parkland. With contour map in hand, go either way around Upper Robin to easily ascend 7144-foot Granite Mountain. Ramble the up-and-down ridge to 6650-foot Trico Mountain. Gaze down upon and/or prowl around nearly two dozen lakes.

Now, the reason we returned the trip to the book: the sermon. What's good for the Enchantments (Hike 20) is good for the Robins—and maybe not good enough, the area being much smaller. Campers absolutely *must not* initiate new patches of bare dirt; camp on established patches of dirt. Wood fires are banned; carry a stove. Do not camp in the middle of the zoo—find privacy in countless nooks on ridges or in adjacent basins. Be careful of the fragile vegetation; where possible walk on bare rock. Camp in this neighborhood of Heaven only when essential to your soul, and not too often; don't be a hog.

78   MARMOT LAKE

Round trip 17 miles
Allow 2 days
High point 4930 feet
Elevation gain 2400 feet
Hikable July through
  September

Map: Green Trails No. 176 Stevens
  Pass
Current information: Ask at Cle
  Elum Ranger Station about trail
  Nos. 1066 and 1376

Sample the variety of the Alpine Lakes: begin with a close-to-the-road and extremely popular valley lake, climb to a cirque lake ringed by cliffs and talus parkland and fishermen, and wander on to a lonesome lake colored jade green by meltwater from a small glacier. Go from forests to heather meadows to moraines. Look up at the peaks from below, then out to the peaks from high viewpoints.

Drive from Salmon la Sac to the Hyas Lake–Deception Pass trailhead, elevation 3350 feet (Hike 75). Hike to Hyas Lake at 1½ miles, 3448 feet. The occupants of most of the scores of cars typically parked at the road-end stop here, content with the wading, swimming, fishing, camping, and looking.

Continue past the lake and along the river bottom, then up switchbacks with views back down to Hyas Lake and across the valley to Mt. Daniel and Mt. Hinman. At 5 miles the trail tops 4475-foot Deception Pass and intersects the Pacific Crest Trail. Turn off it onto trail No. 1066, signed "Marmot Lake, 3½ miles."

The path ascends gently in parkland, by small ponds (camps), crosses a 4760-foot swale in Blue Ridge, and wends down through the meadow basin of Hozzbizz Lake, 4520 feet, beneath scenic cliffs and waterfalls of Peak 6556. The camps here tend to be horsey but several nice sites are in the woods a short way down Hozzbizz Creek. The trail drops to 4100 feet

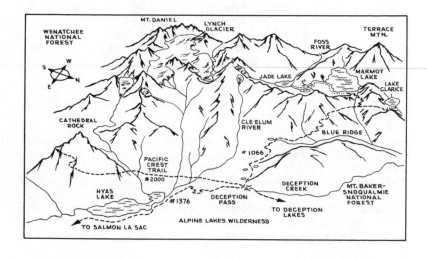

and resumes climbing, crossing a nameless creek from Marmot Lake and at 3 miles from Deception Pass coming to a Y. The right fork leads 1 mile to Lake Clarice, 4530 feet. Switchback left, climbing in a final "Hiker Only" 1/2 mile to Marmot Lake, 4930 feet, 8 1/2 miles. The best camps lie 1/4 mile south along the shore. Until the Forest Service installs privies, watch where you throw down your sleeping bag.

The lake is pleasant to gaze upon, its broad waters mirroring Terrace Mountain, but due to cliffs isn't much for easy exploration. If feeling doughty, carry on. A rough, tricky, awkward path goes up and down around Marmot Lake to the inlet and leads steeply and treacherously up a rocky gully, at a long, slow 1 mile leveling out in the meadow draw of No Name Lake, 5600 feet. A few steps more and—wow!—a bit below, at 5442 feet, lies the miracle of Jade Lake, colored by rock milk from the little Jade Glacier between 7250-foot Lynch Peak on the left and 7960-foot Diptop Peak on the right. A path drops to the lake but to proceed to the far shore and upward on the peaks entails travel beyond what the ordinary hiker should try.

Deception Pass and Marmot Lake also can be approached from the north via Deception Creek or Surprise Lake (Hikes 6 and 7).

Air view of Marmot Lake; Mount Daniel (left) and Mount Hinman (right)

79 RACHEL LAKE– RAMPART RIDGE

Round trip to Rachel Lake 8
  miles
Hiking time 6 hours
High point 4650 feet
Elevation gain 1600 feet
Hikable mid-July through
  October
One day or backpack
Round trip to Rampart Lakes 11
  miles

Hiking time 8 hours
High point 5100 feet
Elevation gain 2300 feet
Hikable mid-July through October
One day or backpack
Map: Green Trails No. 207
  Snoqualmie Pass
Current information: Ask at Cle
  Elum Ranger Station about trail
  No. 1313

A cool and green valley forest, a large alpine lake walled by glacier-carved cliffs that drop straight to the water, a heaven of rock-bowl lakelets and ponds, gardens of heather and blossoms, and ridges and nooks for prowling. On summer weekends hundreds of hikers throng Rachel Lake and dozens are in every pocket and on every knob of the high ridge, where goats and people have woven a spiderweb of paths.

The trail, posted "Hikers Only," was never built but simply beaten into existence by thousands of feet. The way goes around, up, or down to avoid obstacles and hardly knows how to switchback. It will not be improved, will be left as is to help defend against overpopulation.

Drive Interstate 90 east from Snoqualmie Pass 12.5 miles, take Kachess Lake Exit 62, and follow signs 5 miles to Kachess Lake Campground. Turn left 4 miles on Box Canyon road No. 4930 to a junction. Turn left 0.2 mile and hope to find space for your car in the enormous parking lot at the Rachel Lake trailhead, elevation 2800 feet.

The hike begins with a mile of moderate ascent to a rest stop by water-carved and pot-holed and moss-carpeted slabs. The trail levels out along the creek for 1½ miles, passing pleasant little campsites. In an open swath of avalanche greenery, look up to 6032-foot Hi Box Mountain. At 2½ miles the valley ends in an abrupt headwall and rough tread proceeds

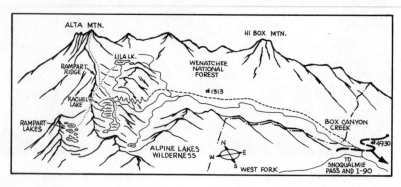

Air view of Rampart Lakes

straight up, rarely bothering to switchback, gaining 1300 feet in a cruel mile, the suffering alleviated by glories of cool-breeze rest-stop waterfalls. Suddenly the angle eases and forest yields to meadows and at 4 miles, 4650 feet, is Rachel Lake.

Follow paths around the lake, admiring blue waters ringed by trees and cliffs—and numerous campsites. Go left past the narrows to the secluded south bay.

To visit higher country, turn right at the shore on a boot-built path climbing above the cirque, with views down to the lake and out Box Canyon Creek. After a steep ½ mile the trail flattens in a wide parkland saddle, 5100 feet, and reaches an unmarked junction offering a choice.

Go right 1 mile to 5200-foot Lila Lake (actually two lakes, or maybe six, plus ponds, scattered about a many-level basin) or walk a tightrope in the sky to (or near) the summit of 6240-foot Alta Mountain.

Go left an up-and-down mile to 5100-foot Rampart Lakes. Savor the little lakes and tiny ponds, the surrounding buttresses and waterfalls. Note the mixture of basalts, conglomerates, and rusty mineralized lobes. Snoop into a flowery corner, climb a heather knoll, think about roaming the short but rough way south to Lake Lillian (Hike 81), and before you know it, arrive on the crest of 5800-foot Rampart Ridge and enjoy views down to Gold Creek, west to Snoqualmie Pass, south to Rainier and Adams, east to Stuart, and north to Three Queens and Chimney Rock.

Camping—Popularity already has forced the exclusion of horses and dogs and the banning of wood fires and waterside camps. How long can the fragile meadowlands survive any camping at all? A permit system seems inevitable—and soon. Actually, it is best not to camp above the valley, confining high-country visits to day hikes. Further, when you find the parking lot full, don't go away mad—try Kachess Ridge (Hike 63).

80 GOLD CREEK

Round trip to Alaska Lake 11 miles
Hiking time 9 hours
High point 4200 feet
Elevation gain 1600 feet
Hikable mid-July through September

One day or backpack
Map: Green Trails No. 207 Snoqualmie Pass
Current information: Ask at Cle Elum Ranger Station about trail No. 1314

Miles of rushing streams, under the steep walls of Rampart Ridge to the east and equally steep cliffs of Kendall Peak to the west. Then rugged paths to either of two alpine lakes—and views—and access to one of the more spectacular sections of the Pacific Crest Trail, the Katwalk. To prevent overuse of the two lakes, the Gold Creek trail has long received minimum maintenance, so expect a few blowdowns to be crawled over or wiggled under. To make more problems: without public notice or meetings, without an environmental impact statement, without permits from any government agency, a corps of four-legged engineers flooded the trail. Detour!

During the season when lingering snow of early summer or premature winter whiteness of September transforms the Katwalk (Hike 83) from easy terrain for a hiker to a tricky path for a trained climber, the alternative is a Gold Creek bypass via Joe Lake.

Drive Interstate 90 east 2 miles from Snoqualmie Pass to Hyak Exit 54. Follow the Forest Service frontage road on the north side of the highway, signed "Rocky Run," 0.8 mile. Cross Gold Creek and turn left on road No. (4832)144. In 0.5 mile go straight ahead and continue about 1 mile, avoiding sideroads to recreation homes, to the well-signed beginning of trail No. 1314, elevation 2600 feet.

The first ⅓ mile is on a gated driveway, the second ⅓ mile on an abandoned road that narrows down to the rough trail traversing the east side

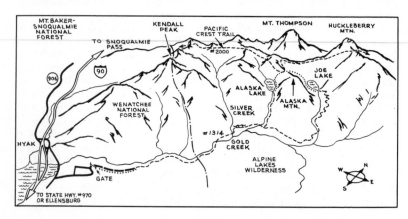

Mount Thompson from Alaska Lake

of the valley, alternating between woods and brush. At 1½ miles enter Alpine Lakes Wilderness. At about 2 miles the trail is blocked by the beaver pond. The best detour is to the left on a big gravel bar. *Beware:* Beyond the pond is a confusion of trails deadending in brush; keep to the right until the trail is found. At about 3 miles cross Gold Creek (on a footlog or by wading) and continue up the west side of the valley, at about 3½ miles crossing Silver Creek. At 3¾ miles is the last of numerous riverside camps. At 4½ miles cross Alaska Creek; ¼ mile beyond, in a tiny, grassy, marshy meadow, find an unmarked junction, 3000 feet. Campsites here and views to Alta Mountain and Chikamin Ridge and Peak.

The left fork climbs 1 steep mile up a tributary through vine maple and slide alder and finally a rockslide to 4200-foot Alaska Lake.

The right fork proceeds up the main valley, contouring and climbing through avalanche greenery, then forest, 1 mile around the base of Alaska Mountain. Traces of the ancient prospectors' path may or may not be found. A steep, hazardous, bootbeaten path on a staircase of rocks and roots continues to the shore of 4624-foot Joe Lake.

81 MOUNT MARGARET– TWIN LAKES–LAKE LILLIAN

Round trip to Twin Lakes
  7 miles
Hiking time 3½ hours
High point 5300 feet
**Elevation gain 1500 feet in, 600
  feet out**
**Hikable late June through
  October**
One day
**Round trip to Lake Lillian
  10 miles**
Hiking time 7 hours

High point 5300 feet
**Elevation gain 1750 feet in, 750 feet
  out**
**Hikable July through
  September**
One day or backpack
**Map: Green Trails No. 207
  Snoqualmie Pass**
**Current information: Ask at Cle
  Elum Ranger Station about trail
  No. 1332**

Climb a little mountain with big views, then proceed in meadows to a pair of lakelets, a basecamp for highland roaming on Rampart Ridge. Thanks (no thanks) to logging on private land, one must walk a steep, rough road that climbs 1000 feet in the first 2 miles.

Drive Interstate 90 east from Snoqualmie Pass 2 miles to Hyak Exit 54. Follow the frontage road on the north side of the highway, signed "Rocky Run." At 2.4 miles, near summer homes, the road becomes No. 4832 and starts abruptly upward. At 3.9 miles go left on road No. 4934. At 4.2 miles are the parking lot and trailhead, elevation 3800 feet.

The land is private (Northern Pacific Land Grant) and so are the roads, which go off in every direction, most of no interest to a hiker. Don't count on signs. Walk watchfully. At 0.2 mile from the trailhead on road No. 4934, go off steeply uphill left on a gated unmarked road. In ⅓ mile keep left; at ⅖ mile go right; at 1 mile keep right; at 1½ miles stay left; and at 1¾ miles reach the road-end, drop a few feet and then climb a boot-beaten path through clearcuts into woods to join what's left of the old Mt. Marga-

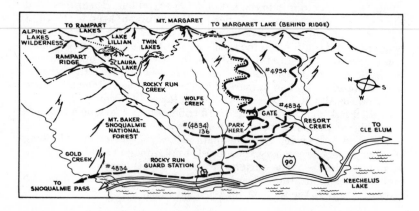

Lake Lillian

ret trail. The ancient tread ascends to a junction at 2½ miles, near a 5100-foot saddle. Turn left. The trail climbs a bit along the crest, then sidehills the west side of Mt. Margaret. For views of Margaret, Stonesthrow, Swan, and Rock Rabbit Lakes (Hike 82), leave the trail and sidetrip to the 5436-foot summit. Having rounded the end of the ridge to the north side of the mountain, the trail descends 600 feet to Twin Lakes, shallow ponds in meadows at 3 miles, 4700 feet; the campsites aren't at all bad.

Now the trail becomes a bit stern. The tread is rough and at times steep as it contours a hillside, losing 150 feet; having entered the Alpine Lakes Wilderness, it then gains 250 feet. At 4½ miles, 4800 feet, is lovely Lake Lillian amid glacier-polished rocks and heather and flowers and alpine trees. The shore slopes are so steep that sleeping space is very scanty.

For off-trail roaming, scramble from the lake to cozy little basins or to broad views atop Rampart Ridge.

82   MARGARET LAKE

Round trip 6 miles
Hiking time 4 hours
High point 5100 feet
Elevation gain 1300 feet in, 300
feet out
Hikable late June through
September

One day or backpack
Map: Green Trails No. 207
   Snoqualmie Pass
Current information: Ask at Cle
   Elum Ranger Station about trail
   No. 1332A

Most lakes in the Alpine Lakes Wilderness are overwhelmed. By contrast, Margaret Lake is relatively ignored. In the immediate neighborhood, for example, the photogenic cirque of Lake Lillian draws hikers by the regiment while demurely lovely Margaret sits lonesome and quiet in parkland and flowers.

Cirquelet-scoops below the east side of Mt. Margaret hold four sparkling lakes—Swan, Rock Rabbit, Stonethrow, and Margaret. Once they were connected by well-kept and much-used trails. But two, Swan and Rock Rabbit, have been made unattractive to hikers by logging. Fortunately, Stonesthrow and Margaret Lakes are protected in the Alpine Lakes Wilderness, but the trail to Stonesthrow has been lost by neglect. However, a good trail still leads to Margaret Lake.

Drive to the Mt. Margaret trailhead (Hike 81), elevation 3800 feet.

Follow the Mt. Margaret route (Hike 81) to the 5100-foot saddle. At the junction go right, switchbacking down. The tread is narrow the first 1/4 mile and then becomes wide as the way enters heather/blueberry meadows of the Alpine Lakes Wilderness. In a scant 1 mile from the saddle, the trail passes shallow, spring-fed Lake Yuanne and a bit farther reaches Margaret Lake, 4800 feet.

Campsites on the south side. Note how monster avalanches have swept down from Mt. Margaret across the lake dumping trees and rocks.

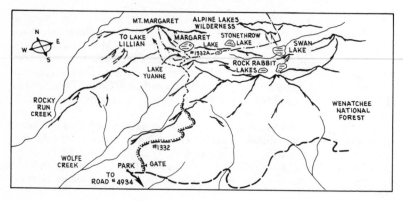

Lake Yuanne and Mt. Margaret

83 KENDALL KATWALK– SPECTACLE POINT

Round trip to Katwalk
10½ miles
Hiking time 7 hours
High point 5400 feet
Elevation gain 2700 feet in, 300
feet out
Hikable mid-July through mid-
October
One day
Round trip to Spectacle Point 31
miles

Allow 3–4 days
High point 5700 feet
Elevation gain 5500 feet in, 3000
feet out
Hikable mid-July through
September
Map: Green Trails No. 207
Snoqualmie Pass
Current information: Ask at North
Bend Ranger Station about trail
No. 2000

The bag of superlatives is quickly exhausted on this, one of the most spectacular parts of the Cascade section of the Pacific Crest Trail, and the most accessible and popular.

Drive Interstate 90 to Exit 52 at Snoqualmie Pass (Exit 53 from the east). Go off the freeway on the Alpental road several hundred feet to the Pacific Crest Trail parking lot, elevation a bit above 3000 feet.

Kendall Peak and The Katwalk

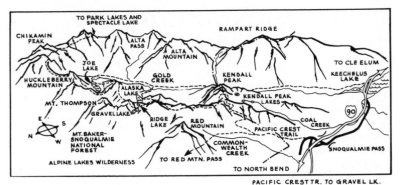

PACIFIC CREST TR. TO GRAVEL LK.

The trail ascends forest 2 miles, loses 250 feet to avoid a boulder field, enters the Alpine Lakes Wilderness, and at 2³/₄ miles passes the Commonwealth Basin trail (Hike 84). Flattening briefly, the way switchbacks endlessly upward, at 4300 feet crosses an all-summer creek that may be the last water until Ridge Lake, and at 4700 feet attains the wooded crest of Kendall Ridge. On a long traverse around the mountain, the path opens out in Kendall Gardens, the start of alpine color that is virtually continuous to Spectacle Point. At 5¹/₄ miles, on a 5400-foot bump, is a happy turnaround for a day hike.

To continue involves stepping carefully along the Kendall Katwalk, blasted across a cliff in solid granite. When snowfree it's safe enough. When snowy, forget it. The mountainside moderates to heather meadows. At 6¹/₂ miles is the 5270-foot saddle between tiny Ridge Lake and large Gravel Lake, the last trail camp until Mineral Creek Park. No fires; carry a stove.

Overnighters based here typically daytrip to Alaska Mountain, 7³/₄ miles, 5745 feet, or to Huckleberry–Chikamin saddle, 10¹/₄ miles, 5520 feet (due to ups and downs, a gross elevation gain of 1100 feet from Ridge Lake). On the way the trail swings around the basins of Alaska Lake and Joe Lake, both 1000 feet below and lacking maintained (or signed) sidetrails. The saddle is a precinct of Heaven but is so fragile that to camp here would be a mortal sin, or at least a capital crime.

The upsy-downsy trail swings across the magnificent cliff-and-meadow face of Chikamin Peak and Four Brothers to a pass overlooking Park Lakes, on the Cascade Crest at 5700 feet, 14 miles. The path descends the alpine basin of Mineral Creek Park to a designated and very pleasant meadow camp at 5200 feet, 14¹/₂ miles, then dips farther to a 4970-foot pass near Park Pond and a junction with the Park Lakes trail (Hike 66). A final ascent of benches and swales tops out at 5475 feet, 15¹/₂ miles, on a shoulder of Three Queens Mountain. Sit on the prow of Spectacle Point jutting out in the sky. Beneath your feet sprawls Spectacle Lake (4350 feet, 2¹/₂ miles down the Crest Trail and then a sidetrail; Hike 64). Across the valley Glacier Lake snuggles in a cirque. Above rises the long rough wall of Four Brothers, Chikamin, Lemah, Chimney Rock, and Summit Chief.

84 COMMONWEALTH BASIN– RED PASS

Round trip to pass 10 miles
Hiking time 5 hours
High point 5400 feet
Elevation gain 2700 feet in, 250 feet out
Hikable mid-July through October

One day or backpack
Map: Green Trails No. 207 Snoqualmie Pass
Current information: Ask at North Bend Ranger Station about trail Nos. 1033 and 2000

The defenders of wilderness who stoutly insisted that Snoqualmie Pass ski areas should not be allowed to groom yo-yo runs on every slope and condos and rathskellers in every valley saved Commonwealth Basin from hyperkinetic recreation and yodeling loudspeakers. Here is the last refuge in the pass vicinity for those who seek quiet enjoyment of the natural scene. The peaceful subalpine forest, the pure and rippling creeks, are an enclave of "olden days" perfect for a family picnic or an experimental backpack.

Drive Interstate 90 to Exit 52 at Snoqualmie Pass (Hike 83). Go off the freeway on the Alpental road and within several hundred feet find the

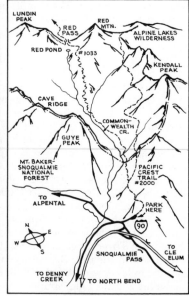

Blueberries

Mount Thompson from Red Pass

Pacific Crest Trail parking lot, elevation something above 3000 feet.

The ancient and honorable trail used to reach the basin in merely 1 mile, but on private land that ultimately was clearcut, causing the old path to erode so severely it was abandoned. The new way takes 2³/₄ miles to make the same distance and in the doing gains 700 feet, of which 250 are lost. But the getting there is the fun, after all.

Follow the Pacific Crest Trail (Hike 83), entering the Alpine Lakes Wilderness in 2¹/₄ miles. At 2³/₄ miles the trail dips near the valley floor before starting up Kendall Ridge. A signed sidepath, trail No. 1033, drops to the old Commonwealth Basin trail. Once on the basin floor go left or right off the trail for picnics—or for camps to try out brand-new gear or new kids.

The basin trail turns upstream 1 mile to the valley head and ascends the crest of an open-forested spur in many, many short switchbacks. At last the way flattens out in heather gardens and alpine trees of a cirque basin at the foot of Red Mountain. A few steps away on a sidetrail is Red Pond, 4¹/₂ miles, 4900 feet. Eat lunch, tour the bouldery and flowery shores, listen for marmots whistling, walk to the edge of the cirque and look over the valley and the rimming peaks and south to Mt. Rainier. Campsites are overused but pleasant; no fires; carry a stove.

The trail swings up talus and rock buttresses almost but not quite to the saddle and follows the ridge west to Red Pass, 5 miles, 5400 feet, and views to the deep Middle Fork Snoqualmie valley, the sharp tower of Mt. Thompson, the rugged Chimney Rock group, and far horizons.

This used to be the official Cascade Crest Trail and descended from the pass to the Middle Fork Snoqualmie River trail (Hike 94); a doughty soul might be able to do it yet.

85 SNOW LAKE–GEM LAKE

Round trip to Snow Lake
  7 miles
Hiking time 6 hours
High point 4400 feet
Elevation gain 1300 feet in, 400
  feet out
Hikable July through
  October

One day or backpack
Map: Green Trails No. 207
  Snoqualmie Pass
Current information: Ask at North
  Bend Ranger Station about trail
  No. 1013

Snow Lake is the largest alpine lake (more than a mile long) near Snoqualmie Pass. On one side rock cliffs rise to Chair Peak, and on the other forested cliffs fall toward the broad, deep gulf of the Middle Fork Snoqualmie River. The trail and lake are overwhelmingly popular—some 14,000 visitors a year, 500 and more on a fine summer Sunday. If it's the sound of silence you're seeking, be warned.

Drive Interstate 90 to Exit 52 at Snoqualmie Pass and go left 2 miles on the Alpental road to the ski area parking lot and the trailhead, elevation 3100 feet.

Trail No. 1013 climbs a bit in forest to intersect the pre-Alpental hiking route, long since obliterated. The way ascends gradually, sometimes in cool trees, sometimes on open slopes with looks over to Denny Mountain, now "Alpentalized," and to The Tooth and Chair Peak, still wild.

At about 1½ miles the way switchbacks a steep mile in heather and flowers and parkland to the saddle, 3 miles, 4400 feet, to Snow Lake. Not until here is the Alpine Lakes Wilderness entered, the entire Source Creek valley having been excluded in order not to discourage free enterprise. Day-hikers may well be content with the picnic spots atop rocks, in blossoms and blueberries, and splendid views. The trail drops sharply ½

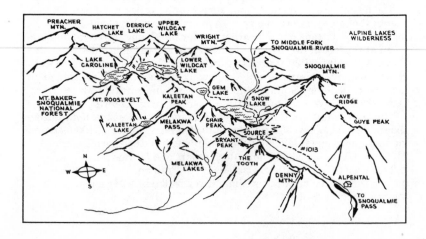

Gem Lake

mile from the saddle to meadow shores of Snow Lake, 3½ miles, 4016 feet, and rounds the east side.

Now, about the camping. Our first advice is don't do it, not here. The Forest Service doesn't say that (not quite yet). However, in order to provide the highest possible quality of experience without limiting the number of visitors, it has devised a management plan for Snow Lake—a plan that informs hikers about "The Responsibility of Freedom." Within a "day-use area" along the shore first reached by trail, hikers are requested not to camp. In the adjoining "heavy-use area," camping must be at established sites only and with no wood fires; carry a stove. So you want to camp free and lonesome? You do best to go someplace else—a place that lacks a lake. However, all around the basin, away from the lake, are private nooks. Get off the trail. Snoop around. Learn how to hide. Don't build fires—the smoke will give you away.

More lakes, more private, lie beyond. Walk the shore ½ mile to where the Rock Creek trail (Hike 95) comes up from the Middle Fork valley and a bit beyond to the creek, which is the lake's outlet. Hereabouts is a confusion of paths, most beaten out by confused hikers and dead-ending at cliffs. To solve the puzzle turn toward the shore, find where the lakeside trail makes a single switchback down to the outlet, and cross on a footlog. At 1½ miles from the outlet is Gem Lake, 4857 feet. Several camps. No fires.

You want still more? The path circles the east shore, climbs a 5000-foot pass, and drops 1000 feet to the two Wildcat Lakes.

86

DENNY CREEK–
MELAKWA LAKE

**Round trip to Melakwa outlet 9
  miles
Hiking time 6 hours
High point 4909 feet
Elevation gain 2300 feet
Hikable mid-July through
  October**

**One day or backpack
Map: Green Trails No. 207
  Snoqualmie Pass
Current information: Ask at North
  Bend Ranger Station about trail
  No. 1014**

The liveliest valley of the Snoqualmie Pass vicinity, a hiker's eyes and ears entertained by a series of waterfalls fluming and splashing. Beyond that excitement is the most spectacular alpine scenery of the pass vicinity, snowfields and cliffs of Kaleetan, Chair, and Bryant Peaks rising above the little lake, which has one shore in forest, the other in rocks and flowers. Walk watchfully to avoid head-on collisions; there is no centerline painted on the trail.

Drive Interstate 90 to Exit 47. Go off on the Denny Creek road, turn right, and continue 3 miles to Denny Creek Campground. Just past, turn left on a road over the river and follow it 0.2 mile, passing private homes, to the road-end trailhead, elevation 2300 feet. Parking is limited; take care not to block driveways.

The trail ascends moderately along Denny Creek in forest, passing under the high bridge of Interstate 90 (keep an eye out for falling trucks), crossing the stream on a bridge at ½ mile, and recrossing at 1 mile, 2800 feet, below water-smoothed slabs of a lovely cataract. The way leaves forest and strikes upward in avalanche greenery to Keekwulee Falls, 1½ miles. The next ½ mile of tight switchbacks ascends around cliffs past Snowshoe Falls. By this point the majority of Sunday strollers have found precisely the perfect spot for a picnic.

The next comparably rich rewards are a good bit farther on. At 2 miles, 3500 feet, the path flattens out in the upper basin, shortly crosses the creek, goes from trees to low brush to trees again, and switchbacks to

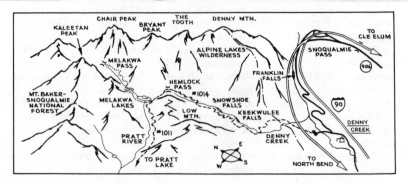

Keekwulee Falls

wooded Hemlock Pass, 4 miles, 4600 feet. The trail drops a bit in forest to
the outlet of Melakwa Lake, 4½ miles, 4550 feet.

Enjoy views of talus, snowfields, and cliffs falling abruptly from the
6200-foot summits of Kaleetan and Chair. The basin is so heavily
pounded it shouldn't be camped in at all; in any event, no fires; carry a
stove. You would be kinder to the fragile basin floor and to yourself to fill
a camping-size water-carrier and clamber elsewhere to find a spot to lay
down your sleeping bag.

For another way back to the highway, and for lonesome walking, take
the 3-mile trail from Melakwa Lake to Pratt Lake (Hike 87).

87 PRATT LAKE

Round trip to saddle 11½ miles
Hiking time 8 hours
High point 4100 feet
Elevation gain 2300 feet in, 700 feet out
Hikable July through October

One day or backpack
Maps: Green Trails No. 206 Bandera and No. 207 Snoqualmie Pass
Current information: Ask at North Bend Ranger Station about trail Nos. 1007, 1009, and 1011

Miles of deep forest lead to a lovely lake amid subalpine trees. A network of trails leads to other lakes and to meadow ridges and high views. Days can be spent exploring from a basecamp here.

Drive Interstate 90 to Exit 47, cross over the freeway, and turn west 0.2 mile to the trailhead parking area, elevation 1800 feet.

The first steep mile of trail No. 1007 gains 800 feet in cool forest to a junction with the Granite Mountain trail. Keep straight ahead and sidehill upward on a gentler grade in young forest, through patches of twinflower, Canadian dogwood, salal, and bracken, by many nurse logs, to Lookout Point, 3 miles, 3400 feet, a much-used camp.

At 3¾ miles is a short sidepath down to Talapus and Olallie Lakes (Hike 89). The main trail rounds the Olallie basin in open subalpine forest to a 4100-foot saddle, 4 miles, a logical turnaround for day-hikers. Lots of huckleberries here in season, plus a view south to Mt. Rainier and a junction with the Mt. Defiance trail (see below). The Pratt Lake trail slants down a steep sidehill with views of Kaleetan Peak and Pratt River valley to the lake's outlet, 5¾ miles, 3400 feet. The once-popular campsites at the outlet have been mostly destroyed by blowdown. In any event, the lake is so heavily used the Forest Service requests campers to stay elsewhere.

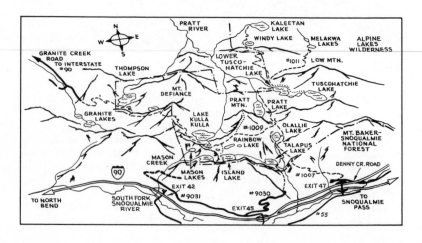

Pratt Lake from Pratt Mountain

Now, for explorations. (These are only a few; connoisseurs of the country have many other private favorites.)

On trail No. 1011, a scant ¹/₂ mile from Pratt Lake, is Lower Tuscohatchie Lake, 3400 feet, and three possible sidetrips: a fishermen's path beats brush 1¹/₂ miles to (Upper) Tuscohatchie Lake, 4023 feet. From the outlet of Lower Tuscohatchie a trail ascends gently, then steeply, 2¹/₂ miles, in trees with glimpses outward of alpine scenery, to 4500-foot Melakwa Lake (Hike 86); from the outlet of Lower Tuscohatchie, a less-used trail climbs northward to 4800 feet and drops past little Windy Lake to Kaleetan Lake, 3900 feet, 3¹/₂ miles. The way to Kaleetan Lake is entirely in forest, with only occasional views over the Pratt River valley, logged in the 1930s, but the lonesome lake has a splendid backdrop in the cliffs of Kaleetan Peak.

From the Olallie–Pratt saddle (see above), the Mt. Defiance trail No. 1009 ascends westward through beargrass and heather and huckleberry meadows (fine views 1100 feet down to Lake Talapus) on the side of Pratt Mountain, whose 5099-foot summit is an easy scramble via huge boulder fields on the southwest side, passes Rainbow Lake (Island Lake lies ¹/₂ mile away on a sidepath and actually is a more rewarding objective than Pratt Lake), comes near Mason Lake, traverses high above Lake Kulla Kulla, and climbs past flower gardens almost to the summit of 5584-foot Defiance, about 3 miles, and broad views (Hike 90). The trail continues westward on the ridge a mile, drops to Thompson Lake, 3400 feet, 5¹/₂ miles, and descends to the Granite Creek road, 7 miles.

88 GRANITE MOUNTAIN

Round trip 8 miles
Hiking time 8 hours
High point 5629 feet
Elevation gain 3800 feet
Hikable July through
 October

One day
Map: Green Trails No. 207
 Snoqualmie Pass
Current information: Ask at North
 Bend Ranger Station about trail
 Nos. 1007 and 1016

The most popular summit trail in the Snoqualmie region, and for good reason. Though the ascent is long and in midsummer can be blistering hot, the upper slopes are a delightful garden of granite and flowers and the panorama includes Mt. Rainier south, Mt. Baker and Glacier Peak north, Chimney Rock and Mt. Stuart east, and infinitely more peaks, valleys, and lakes.

Tragically, this lovely mountain can be a killer. In spring its sunny southwest shoulder melts free of snow very early, deceptively seeming to provide bare-trail access to the heights. But the trail doesn't stay on the shoulder; it crosses a gully where snow lingers late and where climax avalanches thunder to the very edge of the freeway. Hikers "rushing the season" are better advised to climb Bandera (Hike 91).

Drive Interstate 90 to Exit 47, cross over the freeway, and turn west 0.5 mile to the trailhead parking lot, elevation 1800 feet.

The first steep mile on the Pratt Lake trail gains 800 feet in cool forest to the Granite Mountain junction and a creek for resting. This may be the last water.

Go right from the 2600-foot junction, traversing in trees ½ mile, then

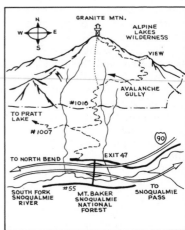

Cloud-filled Snoqualmie River valley

Mount Rainier and Granite Mountain trail

heading straight up and up in countless short switchbacks on an open south slope where fires and avalanches have inhibited the growth of forest. (On sunny days, start early to beat the heat.)

At 4000 feet the trail abruptly gentles and swings east across the avalanche gully—an area of potentially extreme danger perhaps through June. Hikers seeking the summit before July should be very wary of crossing this gully; better to be content with the already very nice views to the south over the Snoqualmie valley to Rainier.

Beyond the gully the trail sidehills through rock gardens, passing a waterfall (early summer only) from snows above, and then switchbacks steeply to grass and flowers, reaching the summit ridge at 5200 feet. In early summer the route beyond here may be too snowy for some tastes; if so, wander easterly on the crest for splendid views over the Snoqualmie Pass peaks, down to alpine lakes, and through the pass to the shores of Keechelus Lake.

The trail ascends westward in meadows, above cozy cirque-scoop benches, and switchbacks to the fire lookout, 5629 feet, 4 miles, and full compensation for the struggle.

It is possible to camp (no fires) near the summit, either for the sunset and dawn views or to allow time for exploration.

The hike has special appeal in early summer when flowers are blooming and in fall when blueberries are ripe and the slopes are flaming.

89 TALAPUS LAKE– OLALLIE LAKE

Round trip to Olallie Lake 4
  miles
Hiking time 3 hours
High point 3780 feet
Elevation gain 1220 feet
Hikable June through
  mid-October
One day or backpack
Map: Green Trails No. 206
  Bandera
Current information: Ask at
  North Bend Ranger Station
  about trail No. 1039

Olallie Lake

A well-groomed forest trail, perfect for first-time backpackers and families with young hikers, leads to two popular lakes with excellent camps and gives access to many more, the area crisscrossed by trails providing infinite opportunity for exploration. Due to the proximity to Puget Sound

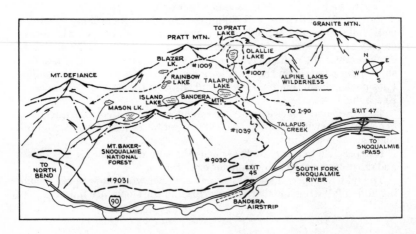

City, weekenders should arrive early to secure a desirable camp—the weekly average is 425 hiker-visits throughout June, July, and August, mostly on weekends.

Drive Interstate 90 to Bandera Airfield Exit 45 signed "Lookout Point." Go off and under the freeway, then straight ahead west 1 mile on road No. 9030 to a split. Go right, uphill, still on road No. 9030, for 3.2 miles to the end at Talapus Lake trail No. 1039, elevation 2560 feet.

The trail begins on an overgrown logging road through an old clearcut, enters forest shade, and in several gentle switchbacks and a long sidehill swing reaches a marshy area just below Talapus Lake. Paths here branch in several directions. The muddy track that stays on the north side of the lake's outlet stream leads to several secluded camps on the west shore. Driest and best-maintained is the main trail, which crosses the outlet on a bridge and at 1¼ miles comes to Talapus Lake, 3200 feet. Forest camps virtually ring the lake. No fires.

The way continues, ascending over a rib ½ mile to meet the sidetrail down from the Pratt Lake trail (Hike 87); turn left ¼ mile to Olallie Lake, 3780 feet, completely wooded, with numerous camps. Also no fires.

To proceed, ascend either by the sidetrail or directly from the far end of Olallie Lake to the Pratt Lake trail (Hike 87). Meadows and views start immediately.

90 MASON LAKE– MOUNT DEFIANCE

Round trip to Mason Lake 5 miles
Hiking time 6 hours
High point 4300 feet
Elevation gain 2000 feet
Hikable June through November
One day or backpack
Round trip to Mt. Defiance 10 miles

Hiking time 10 hours
High point 5400 feet
Elevation gain 3300 feet
Hikable July through October
One day or backpack
Map: Green Trails No. 206 Bandera
Current information: Ask at North Bend Ranger Station about trail Nos. 1009 and 1038

Reasons this hike ought not be in this book at all: a huge and nasty boulder field; a steep, eroded, muddy path—even to call it a trail requires a stretch of the imagination. Any person who makes this trip his first hike most likely never will leave the car again. The nearby Lake Annette and Pratt Lakes trails are much better suited to beginners and families with small children.

Reasons it's in this book after all: it's one of the closest-to-Seattle trails to a mountain lake; despite the horrors, it's short and on a summer day is

Mason Lake trail

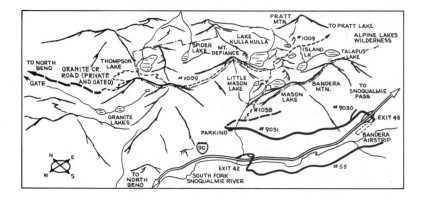

thronged with day-hikers and dogs, young couples carrying babies on backs, and novices with enormous overnight packs; and to give the devil its due, the alpine lakes are numerous and the views from Mt. Defiance tremendous. (Still, the Pratt Lake trail, Hike 87, gets to the same places more sensibly.)

Drive Interstate 90 to Bandera Airfield Exit 45, signed "Lookout Point." Go off the freeway and under it, then straight ahead on road No. 9030. At a split in 1 mile go straight ahead on road No. 9031, signed "Mason Lake Way." At 3.8 miles from the freeway the road is blocked. Park here, elevation 2200 feet.

Ascend the abandoned road about ¾ mile to the torrent of Mason Creek; 300 feet beyond, the sign often hidden by brush, find the Mason Lake trail, which starts out switchbacking upward in fairly decent fashion—and then goes all to pieces. Beaten out by boots with rarely a helping ax or saw, the way goes nearly straight up. At about 1¼ miles the grade eases to cross the boulder field, the route marked (and often mismarked) by a confusion of cairns and plastic ribbons. A final bit of pleasant forest leads to Mason Lake, 4200 feet, 2½ miles. If camps are crowded here, try Little Mason Lake, reached by a swampy sidetrail that also passes a shallow pond. Within a mile are four other lakes. The Pratt Lake trail yields even more.

For views, continue past Mason Lake, climbing 200 feet in ½ mile to a trail junction on the ridge crest between Mason Lake and Lake Kulla Kulla—and signs that suggest a week of explorations. Follow the ridge trail westward, ascending south slopes of Defiance. At 5200 feet, about 2 miles from the junction, traverse a large, steep meadow very near the 5400-foot summit, reached by a steep scramble up the west edge of the flower field. Look north over the Middle Fork Snoqualmie valley to Mt. Baker and Glacier Peak. Look south over the South Fork valley (with freeway) to Mt. Rainier and Mt. Adams.

The trail continues along the ridge, drops to Thompson Lake, then climbs over a spur to the ridge top-to-creek-to-ridge top clearcuts of Granite Creek. If a hiker can arrange for a pickup on the Middle Fork Snoqualmie road, a one-way trip is possible.

91 BANDERA MOUNTAIN

Round trip 7 miles
Hiking time 6 hours
High point 5240 feet
Elevation gain 2800 feet
Hikable mid-May through
October

One day
Map: Green Trails No. 206 Bandera
  (trail not shown)
Current information: Ask at North
  Bend Ranger Station

A boot-beaten track scrambles steeply to the top of Bandera Mountain and superb views down to the freeway-filled valley, south to Mt. Adams and Mt. Rainier, west to Puget Sound country and the Olympics, and north into backcountry highlands of the Alpine Lakes Wilderness. If that isn't enough, add acres of beargrass, whistling (maybe) marmots, and an airplane-wing view of two mountain lakes.

In the summer of 1958 a fire started by loggers swept Bandera to timberline. Long before that, sometime in the nineteenth century, the upper slopes were burned (probably by nature's lightning, not by man's carelessness) and forest has not yet begun to come back. Thus the entire ascent is in the open and can be hot. To compensate, scenery is continuous every step of the way.

Drive to where road No. 9031 is blocked (Hike 90), elevation 2200 feet.

Walk the abandoned road, passing the Mason Lake trail in a long ³/₄ mile. To this point the former road is maintained as trail. Beyond, the Forest Service has allowed alder to grow as thick as hairs on a dog's back. Unless a few volunteers do a bit of lopping and sawing, the old road will become strictly for very skinny people, at least until the young forest begins the usual self-thinning through survival of the fittest. At about 1¹/₂ miles from the parking lot, turn steeply upward ¹/₄ mile on a one-time spur road. At the end of the spur a steep, rutted fire trail hacked out by the Smokey Bears of 1958 heads straight for the sky, first in young trees, over and around downed logs, then climbing 1700 feet in 1 grueling mile,

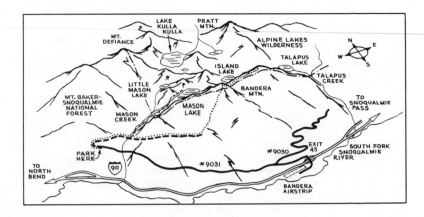

Beargrass and Mount Rainier from Bandera Mountain

made less so by small shrubs and beargrass and picturesque bleached snags from the nineteenth-century blaze. Off to the left, see a lichen-gray granite talus; listen for marmots whistling there and conies squeaking. In a small patch of talus, watch for perfectly preserved tread of an ancient trail. Where did it go? Where did it come from? Who used it? Why?

The ridge crest is attained at around 4700 feet; immediately below on the far side is Mason Lake. The ridge is a good turnaround for those who've had enough; the views are nearly as broad as those from the summit. The route to here often melts free of snow in early May—a safe alternative to Granite Mountain, whose avalanche gully may still be unstable.

Climb east on the crest through subalpine trees, then scramble granite boulders up a step in the ridge to the first summit, 5150 feet, and down-and-up a bit farther to the highest summit, 5240 feet. Look north to lakes in forest bowls below and far away to Glacier Peak and Mt. Baker, northeasterly to Snoqualmie peaks, south down to the highway and beyond to omnipresent Willis Wall of Mt. Rainier, and west past the portal peaks of Washington and Defiance to lowlands. Civilization is near, but also wilderness—the Alpine Lakes Wilderness boundary is just the other side of the ridge.

92 TAYLOR RIVER– NORDRUM LAKE

Round trip to Big Creek 10 miles
Hiking time 5 hours
High point 1700 feet
Elevation gain 500 feet
Hikable June through October
One day or backpack
Round trip to Nordrum Lake 18 miles
Allow 2 days

High point 3700 feet
Elevation gain 2500 feet
Hikable late July through mid-September
Maps: Green Trails No. 174 Mount Si and No.175 Skykomish
Current information: Ask at North Bend Ranger Station about trail Nos. 1002 and 1004

An abandoned logging road, now dwindled to an easy-strolling footroad, and a rough and brushy and slippery and very steep scramble-trail combine to provide a varied experience of forest and rockslide, river and waterfall and subalpine lake. The road-trail is superb for spring and early summer when highlands are miserably white. The lake is the takeoff for some of the lonesomest country in the Alpine Lakes Wilderness.

Drive Interstate 90 east from North Bend, at Exit 34 go off on Edgewick Road, turn left past Ken's Truck Town, then right on Middle Fork Snoqualmie River road No. 56, which in 15.5 miles crosses the Taylor River bridge and turns sharply right. Proceed straight (left) ahead on road No. 5630 3 miles along the Taylor River to the road-end trailhead No. 1002, elevation 1200 feet.

The hike begins by crossing the Taylor River and heading upvalley on the old road, which in 1000 feet splits; stay right, following the river. The

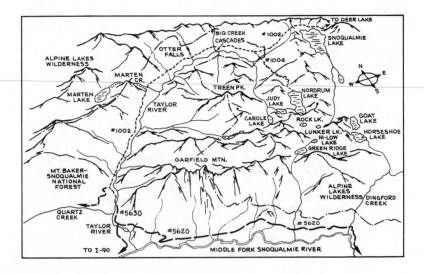

Nordrum Lake

road-trail, which is closed to four-wheel vehicles but not two wheels, can be noisy on summer weekends when the hot sun stirs up the flies and racketeers. It ascends gently in shade of second-growth and stands of virgin forest, passing numerous nice campsites. At 3 miles cross Marten Creek on a little wood bridge; look for a rude path climbing to the falls. In another long mile pause to admire Otter Falls and at 5 miles, 1700 feet, reach the cascades of Big Creek and a heavy-duty concrete bridge, as anomalous as a helicopter in an alpine meadow. Admire the white splash of water over clean granite, perhaps stick a leg or a head in a pool, finish off the cherry tomatoes and granola bars, and turn for home.

Or continue. At 5¾ miles trail No. 1002 ascends left toward Snoqualmie, Deer, Bear, and Dorothy Lakes (Hike 2). In ¼ mile more the road quits at 1800 feet and the Nordrum Lake trail starts, 6 miles from the cars.

At the present time the trail is not maintained. It's a rough start, crossing the river on logs, and gets rougher, aiming straight at the sky up a staircase of rocks and roots that in early summer doubles as a streambed. At 1½ miles (from the road-trail) the way goes over a creek frothing down granite and climbs onward, nearly overgrown by ferns. At 2½ miles the path wanders casually westward beneath a rockslide and ascends slippery granite slabs. The forest opens briefly to views over the Taylor valley to Dog Mountain and lesser summits.

A short descent leads to Nordrum Lake, 4 miles, 3670 feet. To the left is one small camp. For better sites on the west shore round the base of a cliffy hillside, passing an old cabin site.

The lake is the takeoff for backcountry roaming. A rough, boot-beaten path weaves through basins and over saddles to Rock Lake, Lunker Lake, Hi-Low Lake, Green Ridge Lake, and pretty little Quartz Lake.

Lake Dorothy from end of Myrtle Lake trail

MIDDLE FORK SNOQUALMIE RIVER
Alpine Lakes Wilderness

93 MYRTLE LAKE– HESTER LAKE

Myrtle Lake
Round trip 14 miles
Hiking time 7 hours
High point 3777 feet
Elevation gain 2400 feet
Hikable July through October
One day or backpack
Hester Lake
Round trip 12 miles
Hiking time 7 hours

High point 3886 feet
Elevation gain 2500 feet
Hikable July through October
One day or backpack
Map: Green Trails No. 175
    Skykomish
Current information: Ask at North
    Bend Ranger Station about trail
    Nos. 1005 and 1005A

The Dingford Creek trail is a parade of fishing poles, each of the thousands expecting to haul in a share of the hundreds of poor little tame trout trying to dodge the hooks, wishing they'd never been deported from the hatchery. Of the two main fishmarkets, Myrtle Lake has a lot of scenery and people; Hester some scenery and a bit of solitude. The trout-free ridges are lonesome.

Drive Middle Fork Snoqualmie River road No. 56 to the Taylor River bridge (Hike 92) and 6 miles beyond to Dingford Creek trail No. 1005, elevation 1400 feet.

The trail switcbacks steeply 1 mile up second-growth forest dating from logging operations a half-century ago and enters the Alpine Lakes Wilderness, where the grade eases in a cool virgin forest close to the roar of Dingford Creek. At about 3⅓ miles, 2900 feet, the trail splits. The right fork, trail No. 1005A, goes to Hester Lake. For Myrtle Lake go left, staying on trail No. 1005, making a short switchback and then a long upvalley traverse, ascending a moderate grade over a few rough spots and muddy stretches to the lake, 7 miles, 3777 feet. Campsites on both sides of the outlet. For views of Big Snow Mountain take the boot-beaten path leftward around the south shore.

Boots can go where clouds can go. Turn right, over the outlet. The trail shrinks to a path and then, like the Cheshire cat, vanishes altogether in knee-deep brush crisscrossed by windfall. Cross Myrtle's inlet stream to the west side (the USGS incorrectly shows the trail staying on the east side) and proceed upvalley, the trail magically reappearing, quite good though unmaintained. The way switchbacks steeply, passes waterfalls, and at 1 mile from the cirque of Big Myrtle levels off in the upper cirque of Little Myrtle Lake, 4100 feet. In another ½ mile there is a 4500-foot pass at the head of the Miller River and the end of once-upon-a-time-built trail.

For Hester Lake, back at the junction at 3⅓ miles, take the right fork, trail No. 1005A; the trail is in poor shape and will be allowed to stay that way for people wanting a chance to get away from people.

The rude path crosses Dingford Creek, passes a nice campsite, then ascends, moderately at first, in subalpine meadow-marshes and patches of trees, before heading straight uphill to Hester Lake, 6 miles, 3886 feet. The deep blue waters are set in a cirque gouged from 6500-foot Mt. Price; impressive cliffs rise from the shores but leave space for comfortable camps.

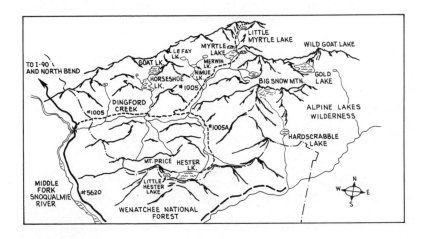

94

MIDDLE FORK SNOQUALMIE RIVER

One-way trip 6¼ miles
Hiking time 3 hours
High point 2200 feet
Elevation gain 800 feet
Hikable May through early
November

One day or backpack
Maps: Green Trail No. 207
Snoqualmie Pass
Current information: Ask at North
Bend Ranger Station about trail
No. 1003

Within the memory of folks still nimbly ambling (or stiffly creaking) about the backcountry a hiker setting out up the Middle Fork hoisted pack at North Bend. Then "lokie loggers" entered the valley with rails and spent a dozen-odd years clearcutting the floor of the glacial trough (and of Pratt River as well), climbing the valley walls as far as a high-line cable could skid logs to a landing. They obliterated most of the trail and caused much of the rest to be abandoned. It was replaced by the CCC Truck Road—built in the 1930s by one of the New Deal's best ideas, the Civilian Conservation Corps.

The Forest Service is planning a modern-times walking route from civilization to headwaters of the Middle Fork. The valley-bottom road, built along the old logging railroad grade in the 1960s to replace the CCC Truck Road, will be paralleled much of the way, yet on the opposite side of the river, far from noise and dust, green and peaceful in second-growth forest getting more old-growth-like each passing decade. The trail will be years in completion, but the 2½-mile segment from Camp Brown will be opened early in the 1990s and the 10-mile segment from Dingford Creek, already finished and described here, is a splendid nearly year-round river-walk. In summer little "beaches" are friendly spots for children to splash around, toss pebbles, and send sticks a-voyaging.

Drive to the Dingford Creek trailhead No. 1005, elevation 1400 feet (Hike 93). Descend the trail, losing 120 feet, and in ¼ mile cross the river

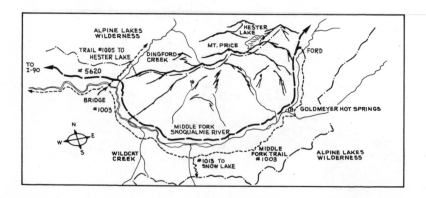

Horse bridge over Middle Fork Snoqualmie River near Dingford Creek

on a sturdy bridge to a junction. Now, a decision: upstream or downstream? Flip a coin or go eeny meeny miney mo or go both ways (one at a time). With a child, downstream probably is best, having more beach as well as views of the Yosemite-like walls of Garfield Mountain. Presently the trail ends in 3½ miles at the edge of private property. In a few years it will be extended to Camp Brown, enabling a one-way (car-assisted) walk.

Upstream, the trail crosses picturesque tributary streams and small groves of virgin forest. The grade is fairly level the 5 miles to Goldmeyer Hot Springs (a private campground, reservations required). The last 1½ miles are steeper, closely following the bellowing river in trees that are the oldest, the mossiest, the greenest, and the tallest to the trail's present end 6½ miles from Dingford Creek. Eventually the route will go another mile to join the Dutch Miller Gap trail (Hike 96).

95 ROCK CREEK–SNOW LAKE

**Round trip to Snow Lake
15 miles
Hiking time 9 hours
High point 4100 feet
Elevation gain 2800 feet
Hikable mid-July through
September**

**One day or backpack
Map: Green Trails No. 207
Snoqualmie Pass
Current information: Ask at North
Bend Ranger Station about trail
Nos. 1003 and 1013**

Since the Cascade Crest Trail moved to Gold Creek to become the Pacific Crest Trail, this portion of the old route has gotten so lonesome that half the tread is soft moss. To be sure, the brush has grown up too; a ½-mile stretch may be real misery and some of the rockslides are less than pleasant. But you'll have Rock Creek to keep you company, 1200 vertical feet of cascades and falls spilling from Snow Lake, and no people to keep you company until the lake. Compared to the approach used by the masses from Snoqualmie Pass, this is 5½ miles longer and gains 1100 feet more elevation. Worth it.

The Rock Creek trail lies across the Middle Fork Snoqualmie River from the road and the Dingford Bridge is the only guaranteed easy way over, though from the road 2.2 miles upvalley from Dingford Creek a crossable logjam may be spotted, but that's chancy. The trip therefore will be described starting at Dingford Creek.

Drive to Dingford Creek trailhead (Hike 93), elevation 1400 feet.

Drop to the valley bottom, cross the river, and hike upstream on the Middle Fork Snoqualmie River trail No. 1003 (Hike 94) 2 miles to the crossing of Rock Creek. At an intersection go right on trail No. 1013. The trail turns uphill, paralleling Rock Creek, then levels off on an old railroad grade. At 2½ miles, 1650 feet, the trail turns uphill again.

Climb to views at 3½ miles, out the Middle Fork valley to Yosemite-like

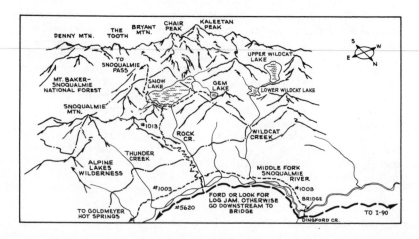

granite walls of Garfield Mountain. At 4½ miles leave second-growth for virgin forest and at 5½ miles look out windows to the Rock Creek headwall and the great waterfall. At 6 miles is a miserable brush-covered rockslide, ending at 6½ miles when the way climbs over a rocky rib to meet the Snow Lake trail, 7½ miles, 4100 feet. The lake is a short walk in either direction; if camping, turn right for the least-mobbed sites.

Snow Lake

96 DUTCH MILLER GAP– LA BOHN GAP

**Round trip to Dutch Miller Gap
15 miles
Allow 2–3 days
High point 5000 feet
Elevation gain 2000 feet
Hikable mid-July through
October
Round trip to La Bohn Gap
approximately 16 miles
Allow 2–3 days**

**High point 5600 feet
Elevation gain 2600 feet
Hikable late July through October
Maps: Green Trails No. 175
Skykomish and No. 176 Stevens
Pass
Current information: Ask at North
Bend Ranger Station about trail
No. 1030**

Hike a glorious valley of forests and meadows and waterfalls, rock-slides and cliffs and jagged peaks, to wilderness headwaters of the Middle Fork Snoqualmie River. Then follow either the main trail to Dutch Miller Gap, named for an early prospector, or a way trail to La Bohn Gap, where he dug his holes in the ground.

Drive Middle Fork Snoqualmie River road to Dingford Creek (Hike 93) and then 6 more miles to the road-end at Hardscrabble Creek, elevation 3000 feet.

The trail enters forest and ascends gently with ups and downs, passing a riverbank camp at 1½ miles.

The transition from low country to high is abrupt: at about 4 miles the trail switchbacks up a step in the valley, going by a splendid cataract of the river, and at the top emerges into heather, grass, flowers, large talus slopes, and views of craggy peaks. The way is flat and frequently marshy and muddy to 6 miles, where the river is so wide and slow and meandering as almost to be a lake, surrounded by a broad meadow. Here, at superbly scenic Pedro Camp, 4100 feet, the trail crosses a branch of the river

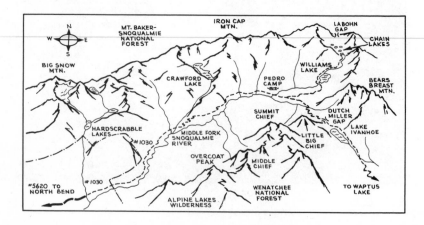

Williams Lake and Little Big Chief Mountain

on a bridge; shortly beyond, prowl around to find remnants of an old miner's cabin (Dutch Miller's?).

The way goes moderately upward in heather and alpine trees another ½ mile to a junction with the Williams Lake–La Bohn Gap trail, an easy ¾ mile to the heather-fringed lake.

For the main event, follow tread a long mile or so from the lake and then climb rockslides and/or snowfields to a magnificent basin of cold little tarns set in granite bowls, of flower patches and waterfalls, and of the mineral outcroppings and diggings and garbage of Dutch Miller's old mine—and of his recent helicoptering successors. Climb a bit more to the 5600-foot crest of La Bohn Gap (2 miles from the junction) and more tarns and views out to Bears Breast Mountain and down to Necklace Valley (Hike 4). Experienced roamers can walk to panoramas from 6585-foot La Bohn Peak west of the gap. Many delightful camps located in the basin and in the gap.

At ½ mile from the Williams Lake junction the main valley trail fords the river, here dwindled to reasonable size, and ascends between the walls of Bears Breast and Little Big Chief, with grand views of Little Big Chief, Summit Chief, Middle Chief, and Overcoat, to the gardens of Dutch Miller Gap, 7½ miles, 5000 feet. Look immediately below to Lake Ivanhoe and out the valley east to Waptus Lake. Look westerly back down the long Snoqualmie valley. The trail drops ½ mile to rock-shored Ivanhoe, 4652 feet, at the foot of the cliffs of Bears Breast. Good camps by the lake. The trail continues down to Waptus Lake and the Cle Elum River (Hike 69).

Night picture of the town of Snoqualmie from Mount Si

MIDDLE FORK SNOQUALMIE RIVER
Mount Si Natural Resources Conservation Area

97   MOUNT SI

**Round trip to Haystack Basin 8
  miles**
Hiking time 8 hours
High point 3600 feet
Elevation gain 3100 feet
Hikable April through November

One day
**Maps: Green Trails No. 174 Mount
  Si and No. 206 Bandera**
**Current information: Ask at
  Enumclaw office of Department
  of Natural Resources**

Climb steeply to the top of a scarp standing awesomely tall at the west
edge of the Cascades. Look down to the Snoqualmie River meandering by
towns and through farms. If the smog isn't too thick, look west to Seattle
and Puget Sound and the Olympic Mountains.

Si is the state's most heavily traveled peak of semi-alpine character.
Mountaineers use the trail for conditioning. Scouts come in troops, and
families with little children, and elderly folk and young lovers and lone
roamers—a cross-section of humanity (in fact, about 10,000 hikers a year)
may be encountered on a typical Sunday.

By May of normal years the way is entirely clear of snow. Sometimes the mountain is briefly bare even in midwinter, and the trail usually can be hiked to high viewpoints in any month.

Drive Interstate 90 to North Bend, take Exit 31 into town, and turn east on North Bend Way, the old highway route. Exactly 1 mile from the east edge of town turn left on 432nd S.E. (Mt. Si Road) and cross the Middle Fork Snoqualmie River. Turn right at the first intersection. Drive 2.5 miles to a parking lot for 175 cars, a picnic area, and the trailhead, elevation 650 feet. The trail is signed "Hikers Only."

The first ½ mile is in alders, then second-growth firs 60–70 years old—except for a 1976 clearcut. At 1 mile is a vista point on a big rock alongside the trail. At 1¾ miles enter Snag Flat, a green twilight of old snags killed by fires and huge living firs, some 8 feet in diameter, that survived the flames. Water here about 200 feet off the main trail on a spur.

The trees get smaller but views are scarce until the old trail is intersected at 3 miles, just below the ridge, a mile from the top. The way then follows a rocky shoulder to Haystack Basin, at the foot of the cliffs of the final peak.

People who have never climbed any mountain whatsoever often feel driven by curiosity or ego to continue to the summit of the Haystack, 4167 feet. The scramble-gully is steep enough to give a flatlander the sort of nervous fit that causes rocks to be dislodged to bound down the gully; when wet it is tremendously slippery and when snowfilled demands mountaineering skills. Under the best of conditions the danger is great of being skulled by the rocks kicked loose by those nervous scramblers and some danger, when they go catatonic, of being fallen upon by human bodies. The summit view is only slightly better than that from the basin.

Much of the mountain is in the Mt. Si Natural Resources Conservation Area, one in a system of preserves (presently numbering twenty-one) that by 1991 action of the state legislature have been set aside from the former mandatory requirement of commodity production, the new emphasis being the protection of gene pools, water quality, native plants, wildlife habitat, unique natural features, scenery, and the provision of *low-impact* recreation. Mt. Si thus has a status similar to that of the Alpine Lakes Wilderness.

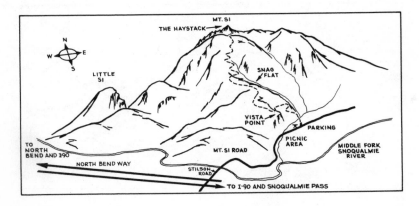

98   BARE MOUNTAIN

Round trip 8 miles
Hiking time 6 hours
High point 5353 feet
Elevation gain 3250 feet
Hikable late June through
  October

One day
Maps: Green Trails No. 174 Mount
  Si and No. 175 Skykomish
Current information: Ask at North
  Bend Ranger Station about trail
  No. 1037

A lonesome trail up a green hillside to a former fire lookout with panoramic views north to Mt. Baker and south to Mt. Rainier and west to the Olympics. So little-walked is the path that the tread is grown up in moss and grass—and may be lost under a canopy of flowers and bracken.

Drive Interstate 90 to North Bend, take Exit 31 into town and onto the main street, the former highway. Go two blocks east of the stoplight and turn north on Ballaratt Street, which leads to North Fork County Road. At 4 miles from North Bend is a Y; take the left, uphill, perhaps signed "Lake Hancock." In 7.5 miles pass the Lake Hancock junction ("Spur 10") and proceed onward. At about 21 miles enter national forest, the road now becoming Lennox Creek road No. 57. Just beyond the boundary the road forks; go left crossing Lennox Creek, and then right. Twenty-three miles from North Bend (what with all the chuckholes on the county segment, allow an hour for the drive) is the trailhead, signed "Bare Mountain trail No. 1037." Park here, elevation 2100 feet.

The first 2 miles follow an abandoned mining road, rock-hopping Bear Creek near a beautiful pool. (Note: It's "Bare" Mountain and "Bear" Creek. Were they named for two different reasons?) In ³/₄ mile the way recrosses the creek on a footbridge, enters the Alpine Lakes Wilderness, and climbs another ¹/₄ mile to a large meadow covered with waist-high bracken. Find the trail with your feet—but watch out for hidden holes! At about 2 miles from the car may be a small white post obscurely marking a

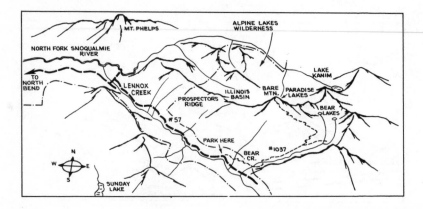

Glacier Peak from Bare Mountain

junction, 3650 feet. Go left. (The right fork dead-ends at an old mining claim. If after crossing the large meadow you enter forest, you are ¼ mile beyond the junction on this, the wrong way.)

The left (correct) fork sets out from the junction so deep under ferns the boots can feel it but the eyes can't see it. Eventually, though, the path emerges in the open and after gaining 1700 feet in 46 switchbacks attains the 5353-foot summit.

All that remains of the lookout cabin, which was removed in 1973, is broken glass, rusting cables—and a grand view.

The three Paradise lakes sparkle below, a tempting 1000-foot dive; due to formidable cliffs, this seems the only way to get there from here.

99   LENNOX CREEK

**Round trip to Anderson Lake 7¼
  miles**
Hiking time 5 hours
High point 4600 feet
**Elevation gain 1900 feet in, 400
  feet out**
**Hikable July through early
  November**

One day or backpack
**Maps: Green Trails No. 174 Mount
  Si and No. 175 Skykomish**
**Current information: Ask at North
  Bend Ranger Station about trail
  No. 1001**

Waterfalls, broad slopes of heather meadows, views of peaks and valleys, and a quiet lake—all in a little-traveled portion of the Cascades. After lying in limbo 30 years, this trail was reopened in 1970, hikers began
to discover the beauties of the North Fork Snoqualmie, and as a conse-
quence the Alpine Lakes Wilderness boundaries were drawn to preserve
some of them. The trail has received minimum maintenance and alternates between good original tread and rough-and-tumble rocks and roots.

Drive from North Bend about 21 miles on the North Fork County Road
(Hike 98) to the boundary of Mt. Baker–Snoqualmie National Forest,
cross Lennox Creek, and turn right at the first fork. From the boundary
drive 4 miles, passing the Bare Mountain trail (Hike 98) to two small
bridges over island-divided channels of Lennox Creek. About 0.2 mile farther is a fork; keep right (straight ahead) on road No. (5700)210,
switchbacking up Cougar Creek drainage a scant mile to the road-end at
a hogback, elevation 2700 feet.

The trail starts steeply up the hogback on a bulldozer track, in less
than ¼ mile going from logged barrens into forest. The way then contours
the east side of Dog Mountain, traversing shoulders of a large avalanche
chute. At about 2 miles the route enters a land of heather laced by numerous creeklets. Directly below the meadows and a bit hard to see is the
spectacular waterfall of one of the tributaries of Lennox Creek.

At about 3¼ miles, 4600 feet, the trail gains a wooded saddle in the

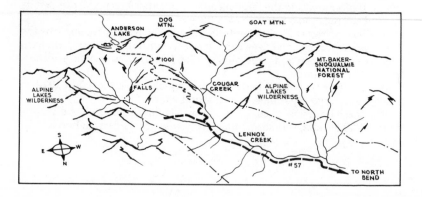

ridge. Enjoy the views down to Taylor River and across the valley to Treen Peak and a most unfamiliar aspect of Garfield Mountain.

The formal trail ends at the saddle but a boot-beaten path drops 400 feet in a rough ½ mile to little Anderson Lake, surrounded by patches of heather and a lot of trees. Camping is nice and quite private but wood is scarce.

Snowpatches in July on Lennox Creek trail

|OO PACIFIC CREST TRAIL

One-way trip between Snoqualmie Pass and Stevens Pass 67 miles
Allow 5 days minimum
High point 5800 feet
Elevation gain about 10,600 feet
Hikable mid-July through mid-September

Maps: Green Trails No. 176 Stevens Pass, No. 207 Snoqualmie Pass, and No. 208 Kachess Lake
Current information: Ask at Mt. Baker–Snoqualmie National Forest information office about trail No. 2000

The segment of the Mexico-to-Canada Pacific Crest National Scenic Trail between Snoqualmie Pass and Stevens Pass traverses the complete south–north width of the Alpine Lakes Wilderness, sampling superb scenery of the Cascade Crest, highland flower gardens, deep-shadow virgin

Two Hyas lakes and (across valley) Pacific Crest Trail passing Cathedral Rock

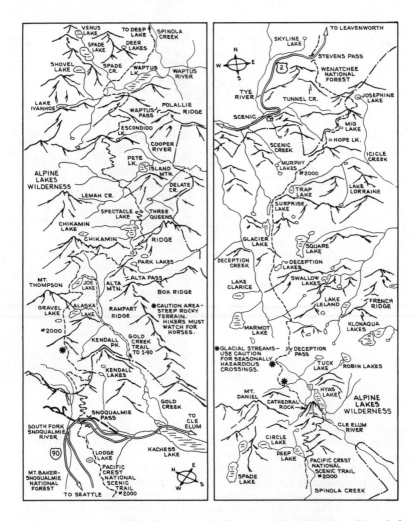

forests, lakes, waterfalls, the peace that surpasseth, all on a well-graded trail with numerous choice camps and a lifetime of sidetrips.

Close to Puget Sound City and population centers of Central Washington as it is, and drawing wilderness lovers from across the nation, the trail is among the most popular in America. To guard the fragile meadows, lakeshores, and streambanks from excessive wear and tear, hikers must be gentle, camping only in designated, established sites or well away (say, 1/4 mile or more) from the trail, and faithfully observing the principles of no-trace camping.

The following is a summary of the route; for more detail and exact mileage logs consult the Forest Service map, available at any office. From Stevens Pass the trail continues 185 miles north to Allison Pass in

231

Canada (see *100 Hikes in the Glacier Peak Region* and *100 Hikes in the North Cascades*), and from Snoqualmie Pass, 97 miles south to the Columbia River (see *100 Hikes in the South Cascades and Olympics*).

Obviously, the trip can be done in either direction and is described here from south to north for no particular reason. A favorite strategy is to do it one way, having some benefactor provide the drop-off and pickup. An important reason hikers are drawn from great distances is the availability of public transportation at both ends of the trail, permitting a group (say) to fly from Detroit to Seattle, catch a bus to one pass or another, catch another bus back to Seattle, and fly home, leaving the driving to them.

Drive Interstate 90 east to Snoqualmie Pass, go off on Exit 52, cross under the freeway, and on the first right proceed uphill to the Pacific Crest Trail No. 2000 parking area, elevation slightly above 3000 feet.

The way climbs high on Kendall Peak (Hike 83) and ridge-runs meadows to Ridge Lake and the first campsites, 6 miles. (Note: Snow lingering late on the Kendall Katwalk may force through-hikers to detour from or to Snoqualmie Pass via Joe Lake and Gold Creek, Hike 80.) It goes by the first designated camp at Ridge and Grand Lakes and makes a great near-contouring swing around the head of Gold Creek's glacial trough, passing above Alaska and Joe Lakes, sidehilling garden slopes of Alaska and Huckleberry Mountains and Chikamin Peak, and drops to the next designated camps at 15 miles, on a meadow ridge above Park Lakes.

Ascend parkland to the grand views from Spectacle Point (Hike 83) on a shoulder of Three Queens Mountain and drop to Spectacle Lake junction (Hike 64), 17 miles; camps are abundant at the lake and along the creek. Continue mainly downhill 4 miles to the next camp at the crossing of Lemah Creek. Other camps are near the Pete Lake trail junction, at the start of switchbacks ascending a shoulder of Summit Chief Mountain, and before and after Escondido Ridge Tarns, 27 miles. Pass above Escondido Lake at 27½ miles, the Waptus Burn trail, another camp, and drop to cross the Waptus River, 32 miles. Round Waptus Lake to an excellent camp at Spade Lake trail and a split in the trail; either climb high across open-forested slopes or round the lakeshore to many popular camps (Hikes 69 and 70); the paths rejoin on the long ascent of Spinola Creek, passing more camps, to Deep Lake (Hike 75), 39 miles.

Bears Breast Mountain and Mount Hinman from Pacific Crest Trail

Switchback up from the deep cirque to Cathedral Pass, 42½ miles, and roll down and up slopes of Cathedral Rock and Mt. Daniel to Deception Pass (Hike 75), 47½ miles. (Note: Two tumbling streams below Daniel are so hazardous in early-summer snowmelt and fall cloudbursts that hikers often are forced to detour from Cathedral Pass to Deception Pass via Squaw Lake and Hyas Lake; watch for warning signs at the junctions.) Camps are about a mile west of Deception Pass on the Marmot Lake trail (Hike 78).

Swing on the near-level around the head of Deception Creek to Deception Lakes (Hike 7) and camps, climb the side of Surprise Mountain to Pieper Pass, and drop to Glacier Lake, 54¼ miles. Ascend forest to a parkland pass, drop to Trap Lake, traverse a meandering ridge, and drop to limited camps in the huckleberry meadows of Hope Lake and then Mig Lake (Hike 8). Descend to a wooded pass, regain the ridge, and pass near Swimming Deer Lake (Hike 9), 62½ miles. Swing around the cirque above Josephine Lake, through a saddle, and down to Lake Susan Jane and the last (first) camps; proceed out of the Alpine Lakes Wilderness and under powerlines of upper Mill Creek, then down the ski area to the trailhead parking at Stevens Pass, 67 miles.

ALTERNATIVE TRAILS

NONWILDERNESS TRAILS IN THE ALPINE LAKES REGION

As major wilderness trails grow thronged, the lesser become attractive; as even the lesser become overpopulated, the brush begins to look good. Thanks to most hikers being content to stay safely and sanely on well-maintained tread, getting as little as ¼ mile from the likes of the Pacific Crest Interstate Freeway (Pacific Crest Trail) may suffice to escape the thud of boots, the roar of backpacker stoves, and the crunching of freeze-dried shrimp and the slurping of portable soup. When your favorite Alpine Lakes Wilderness trail is crowded and the camps along it are being trampled to death, explore elsewhere. For the following alternate hikes, either find directions in other guidebooks or obtain the appropriate maps and let your imagination and feet run wild.

SKYKOMISH RIVER

West Fork Miller River. 4½-mile hike on an abandoned road, now a pleasant streamside trail in forest of cliff-walled valley. (See *Footsore 2* .)

Lake Isabel. 4½-mile road-walk and boot-beaten path to Lake Isabel, a blue gem in a deep cirque of Ragged Ridge. (See *Footsore 2.*)

Barclay and Eagle Lakes. 2¼-mile trail to popular Barclay Lake under the terrifying north face of Mount Baring and a steep boot-beaten path another 2¼ miles to Eagle Lake. (See *100 Hikes in Washington's Glacier Peak Region.*)

Scorpion Mountain. A difficult 4½-mile climb to lovely alpine meadows and views. (See *100 Hikes in Washington's Glacier Peak Region.*)

Evergreen Mountain. 4½ miles to a fire lookout with spectacular views of the Monte Cristo Range.

Sultan Basin DNR Trails. 2-mile trail to the two delightful Greider Lakes, and a 4-mile trail to Boulder Lake with meadows, forest, and campsites. (See *100 Hikes in Washington's Glacier Peak Region.*)

NASON CREEK

Lanham Lake trail No. 1589. 1¾ miles to a shallow lake under cliffs of Jim Hill Mountain. Crosses a powerline road and parallels a logging road ½ mile.

Nason Ridge. Five nonwilderness trails on the north side of Stevens Pass Highway. 4½ miles up Snowy Creek to Rock Mountain. A steep 5½ miles up the Rock Mountain trail. 3 miles to popular Merrill Lake. 5 miles to Alpine Lookout. A 16-mile traverse of Nason Ridge. (All described in *100 Hikes in Washington's Glacier Peak Region.*)

MISSION CREEK

Magnet Creek trail No. 1206. 3-mile connector between US 97 and Tiptop–Mt. Lillian trail No. 1204. Motorcycle country but this steep trail gets no ORV use.

Squilchuck trail No. 1200. 2-mile hike in alpine forest. Access to Marion

Lake, surrounded by meadows, forest, and an ancient lava flow. A few good campsites. Little motorcycle use.

SWAUK PASS AREA

Tronsen Meadow trail No. 1205. 1½ miles between road No. (7240)411 in Tronsen Meadow and road No. 9712 in Upper Haney Meadow. Moderate ORV use.

Ridge trail No. 1352. 4 miles from road No. 213 to Table Mountain road No. 3500. Trail follows ridge between First Creek and Boulder Creek. Moderate 4x4 use.

Nealy Creek trail No. 1370. 3¼-mile trail from Table Mountain road No. 35 to forest boundary. Trail poorly defined in open. Light use by motorcycles and 4x4s.

Naneum–Wilson trail No. 1371. 6½-mile trail mainly in timber. Access from Table Mountain road No. 35. Light motorcycle use.

Drop Creek trail No. 1371A. Access trail from road No. 35 to Naneum–Wilson trail No. 1371. Light motorcycle use.

Owl Creek trail No. 1389. 1¾-mile access from Table Mountain road No. 35 to Naneum–Wilson trail No. 1371. Light motorcycle use.

First Creek trail No.1374. 4¼-mile trail used as a stock driveway from the Green Canyon road to Ridge trail No. 1352. Light motorcycle use.

Wilson Creek trail No. 1387. 5 miles from Table Mountain road No. 2008 to the forest boundary. Light motorcycle use.

Regan trail No. 1354. 4¼-mile trail over Basalt Bluff with several viewpoints over Naneum Creek. To reach Regan trail take Nealy Creek trail No. 1370, then Naneum–Wilson trail No. 1371. Open to motorcycles, use unknown.

TEANAWAY RIVER AREA

Snowshoe Ridge trail No. 1368. 2½-mile trail following open areas along Snowshoe Ridge from road No. 3507 to Table Mountain road No. 35. Light motorcycle use.

Standup trail No. 1369. 6-mile climb to views of Stuart Range, joining trail No. 1391.1 below Earl Peak and ending at Stafford Creek trail No. 1359 (Hike 45) 1 mile from County Line Trail. Closed to motorized vehicles.

CLE ELUM RIVER

West Fork Teanaway River trail No. 1353. 9½-mile trail from road No. 113 up the West Fork Teanaway River to Jolly Mountain trail No. 1307. Several difficult river crossings. Light motorcycle use.

Jolly Creek trail No. 1355. 4-mile access from forested Middle Fork Teanaway trail No. 1393 to open meadows of Jolly Mountain trail No. 1307. Light motorcycle use.

Way Creek trail No. 1235. Steep ½-mile descent from Jungle Creek road No. 9701 to Middle Fork Teanaway River trail No. 1393. Way Creek access bypasses seven crossings of the Middle Fork River. Trail not maintained. Light motorcycle use.

Jungle Creek trail No. 1383A. 4½-mile trail from Jungle Creek road No. 218 over a forested ridge to the Johnson Creek trail. Trailhead is difficult to locate. Light motorcycle use.

Sasse Mountain trail No. 1340. 9-mile sheep driveway along ridge tops from Hex Mountain to Jolly Mountain. Starts from road No. (4305)116, ends at trail No. 1307. Some parts of this trail are closed to motorcycles.

Hex Mountain trail No. 1343. Steady 1½-mile climb from road No. 116 to the open summit of Hex Mountain and Sasse Mountain trail No. 1340. Moderate motorcycle use.

Red Mountain trail No. 1330. 7-mile trail with great views connecting to the Kachess Ridge trail a mile short of Thorp Mountain Lookout (Hike 61). Alternate access to Red Mountain possible off spur road from Cooper Pass; abandoned trail follows ridge to meet trail No. 1330. No motorcycle use.

Paris Creek trail No. 1393.1. 8 miles to open basin where trail is difficult to follow. One could spend a week here without retracing the path, since the trail joins the Teanaway, Jolly Mountain, and Boulder–De Roux trails. Motorcycle country.

Fortune Creek–Van Epps Pass trail No. 4W302. Jeep "trail" to pass, and at 2½ miles, to old mining camp. Trail continues, very obscure, to Solomon Creek trail.

SNOQUALMIE PASS

Guye Peak. Rough trail from Alpental ski area to saddle between Guye Peak and Snoqualmie Mountain.

Snoqualmie Pass Ski Area. Follow the Cascade Crest Trail southward through the ski area to views south to Mt. Rainier and north to the Alpine Lakes Wilderness.

Lake Annette. 3½ miles to lovely forested lake. No solitude here but lots of campsites. (See *100 Hikes in Washington's South Cascades and Olympics.*)

Silver Peak. 4 miles to great views. (See *100 Hikes in Washington's South Cascades and Olympics.*)

McClellan Butte. 4½ miles to views. (See *100 Hikes in Washington's South Cascades and Olympics.*)

Mount Washington. 5-mile walk on gated road to grand views of the Puget Sound country. (See *Footsore 2.*)

MIDDLE FORK SNOQUALMIE RIVER

Mount Teneriffe. 7 miles up a gated jeep road from the valley and then ¾-mile trail to summit. (See *Footsore 2.*)

Pratt River. 7 miles to Pratt Lake but until the bridge is built must first ford the Middle Fork Snoqualmie River.

Rainy Lake trail (not a trail) from Camp Brown. Route very difficult to find. 6 or 7 hours to lake.

Quartz Creek. Gated logging roads followed by a very difficult ¾-mile fishermen's trail to Blethan Lake.

NONWILDERNESS TRAILS
DESCRIBED IN THIS GUIDEBOOK

Icicle Ridge, trail No. 1570, Hike 19—ORVs prohibited

Red Hill, trail No. 1223, Hike 36—Moderate ORV use, closed to ORVs November to June 15

Mission Ridge, trail No. 1201, Hike 37—Heavy motorcycle use

Devils Gulch, trail No. 1220, Hike 38—Heavy motorcycle use

Mt. Lillian Loop, trail Nos. 1372 and 1381, Hike 40—Closed to ORVs until June 15, then light use

Tronsen Ridge, trail No. 1204, Hike 41—Moderate motorcycle use

Three Brothers, trail No. 1211, Hike 42—Motorcycles prohibited

Blewett Ridge, trail No. 1226, Hike 43—Moderate motorcycle use

Iron Creek–Teanaway Ridge, trail Nos. 1351 and 1364, Hike 44—Moderate motorcycle use

Navaho Pass, trail No. 1359, Hike 45—Motorcycles prohibited

Miller Peak, trail No. 1379, Hike 46—Moderate motorcycle use

Bean Creek Basin, trail Nos. 1391 and 1391a, Hike 47—Motorcycles prohibited

Medra Pass, trail No. 1383, Hike 50—Light motorcycle use

Gallagher Head, trail No. 1392, Hike 51—Little motorcycle use but considerable ORV use at lake

Esmerelda Basin, trail No. 1394, Hike 56—Motorcycles prohibited

Longs Pass, trail No. 1229, Hike 58—Motorcycles prohibited

Koppen Mountain, trail No. 1392.1, Hike 52—Motorcycles prohibited

Iron Peak, trail No. 1399, Hike 53—Motorcycles prohibited

Middle Fork Teanaway, trail No. 1393, Hike 57—Moderate motorcycle use

Yellow Hill–Elbow Peak, trail No. 1222, Hike 58—Light motorcycle use

Thorp Lake trail No. 1316, Hike 59—Motorcycles prohibited

Little Joe Lake, Hike 60—Motorcycles prohibited

Thorp Mountain, trail No. 1315, Hike 61—Motorcycles prohibited

French Cabin Mountain, Hike 62—Illegal motorcycle use on trail Nos. 1307 and 1315; trail No. 1308 is open to motorcycles but gets no such use

Kachess Ridge, trail No. 1315, Hike 63—Some illegal motorcycle use

INDEX

The MOUNTAINEERS, founded in 1906, is a nonprofit outdoor activity and conservation club, whose mission is "to explore, study, preserve, and enjoy the natural beauty of the outdoors..." Based in Seattle, Washington, the club is now the third-largest such organization in the United States, with 12,000 members and four branches throughout Washington State.

The Mountaineers sponsors both classes and year-round outdoor activities in the Pacific Northwest, which include hiking, mountain climbing, ski-touring, snowshoeing, bicycling, camping, kayaking and canoeing, nature study, sailing, and adventure travel. The club's conservation division supports environmental causes through educational activities, sponsoring legislation, and presenting informational programs. All club activities are led by skilled, experienced volunteers, who are dedicated to promoting safe and responsible enjoyment and preservation of the outdoors.

The Mountaineers Books, an active, nonprofit publishing program of the club, produces guidebooks, instructional texts, historical works, natural history guides, and works on environmental conservation. All books produced by The Mountaineers are aimed at fulfilling the club's mission.

If you would like to participate in these organized outdoor activities or the club's programs, consider a membership in The Mountaineers. For information and an application, write or call The Mountaineers, Club Headquarters, 300 Third Avenue West, Seattle, Washington 98119; (206) 284-6310.

Send or call for our catalog of more than 200 outdoor books:
The Mountaineers Books
1011 SW Klickitat Way, Suite 107
Seattle, WA 98134
1-800-553-4453